SEAN MESSER: AGE 42 DEAD ON ARRIVAL

The shame of San Francisco: Sean Messer spent Years screaming for help and now he's dead.

By Al Saracevic Examiner columnist Aug 25, 2022, Updated Aug 2022

I heard him most every day around noon, yelling and screaming at the top of his lungs in the alley below my office window. It was "F this" and "F that" and other choice words, a stream of profanity spilling forth from his troubled mind.

He was clearly in need of help, wandering the Financial District and North Beach for years, self-medicating and telling all the world of his dire need for mental health services.

In San Francisco, those cries for help fell on deaf ears.

On the morning of Wednesday, Aug. 10, police answered a call about an unresponsive man on Commercial Street. That's where they found Sean Messer, age 42, address unknown. He had died alone on a parklet in front of a Chinese restaurant.

Shouting Out!

Homeless, addicted, mentally Ill

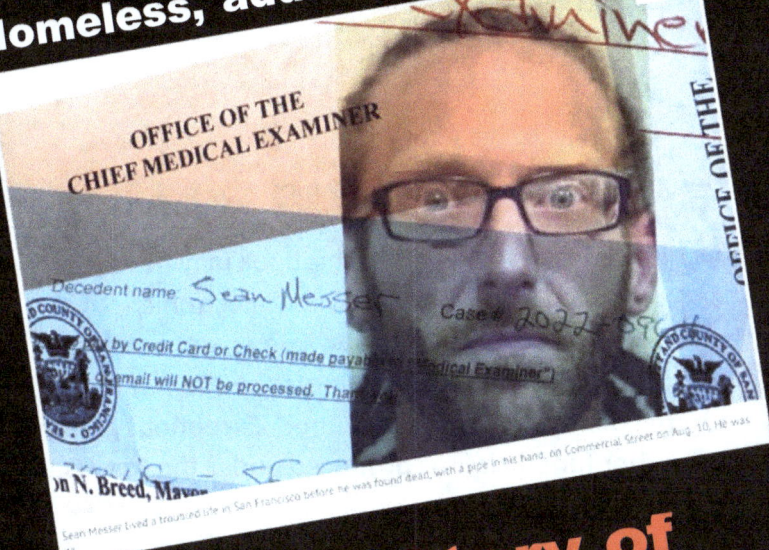

OFFICE OF THE
CHIEF MEDICAL EXAMINER

Decedent name *Sean Messer*

Case # *2022*

by Credit Card or Check (made payable to *Medical Examiner*)

email will NOT be processed. Thank you

on N. Breed, Mayor

Sean Messer Lived a troubled life in San Francisco before he was found dead, with a pipe in his hand, on Commercial Street on Aug. 10. He was

A True Story of Tragedy and HOPE

By Jan Cosmos

Inquiries: Seanmesser820@gmail.com

Purchase: Additional copies may be purchased at Parsonsporch.com and Amazon.com or by calling Parson's Porch Books at 423.310.8815.

COPYRIGHT © 2023

And now, the streets and alleys of the Financial District have gone quiet.

I asked the security guard in our building about this poor soul, and he knew exactly who we were talking about.

"He would come around about lunchtime, and then cuss out everyone or cuss in the general area of everyone. He wasn't really cussing *at* anyone," said Dave Carter, who mans the desk at the Merchants Exchange Building on California Street. "One time, when I went out and talked to him about making too much noise.

He broke down crying, saying, 'I got problems, I got problems' over and over. He really wasn't a disagreeable guy."

No, he was a mentally ill guy who desperately needed help

… which never arrived.

And this is the shame of San Francisco.

Messer was one of hundreds, if not thousands, of seriously sick individuals who walk our streets on a daily basis. We all see them. We all hear them, muttering or yelling or crying out loud. Yet there's not much done for the Sean Messers of the world. They are left to fend for themselves. And the end is often tragic.

San Francisco's Office of the Chief Medical Examiner confirmed Messer's death, but I'm still waiting on the full toxicology report. Talking to people around the neighborhood who were there that day, they say he died with a pipe in his hand.

If true, that would make him one of hundreds who die under similar circumstances in San Francisco every year. From January through July of this year, 88 people with no fixed residence died from overdose in The City, according to statistics obtained from the Chief Medical Examiner.

And this is the shame of San Francisco.

I asked some local beat cops if they knew Messer, and they did. They had heard the news and weren't surprised. He was a regular on the streets, and they had calmed him down in the past. But they didn't really have anywhere to take him. They told me anyone taken to San Francisco General Hospital is released way before the 72-hour limit on psychiatric holds. Patients are released even quicker from St. Francis Hospital, on Hyde Street.

Sadly, amazingly, shockingly considering our homeless spending budget, there's really nowhere to take mentally ill homeless people in San Francisco. And the police are at wits' end. It all speaks to the desperate need for a statewide mental health system, funded with help from the feds. The problem is just too big for San Francisco to solve on its own.

Fady Zoubi, who works at U.S. Bank at the intersection of California and Montgomery, knew Messer for years. He would see him ranting in the streets and offer him a cigarette. "It would calm him down," said Zoubi. "He could be very nice. But he would say things like the electricity in the air was hurting his brain, things like that. He needed mental health care."

I talked to the shopkeepers on Commercial Street, a charming little alley that runs from Sansome to Grant and used to house sidewalk cafes reminiscent of Europe. The restaurant owners kept the street clean to attract customers. But the San Francisco Fire Department cracked down on the tables and chairs just before the pandemic, for unclear reasons. It's gone downhill ever since. Homeless sleep in the doorways and on the sidewalks at night. People like Sean Messer.

"We are so fed up with the situation," said Alfred Schilling, who owns Schilling & Co. Cafe right across the street from where Messer was found. "You know I feel very sorry for these people. I see a regular lady, who is probably around 50, sleeping in the doorway over there. Why can't we help these people? You know it is shameless. We make them live like animal and nobody do anything."

I asked if he's called City Hall for help, and he laughed in my face. "Who calls the city? Please. ... You need good management, OK? I don't know the mayor. But they all should be fired, in my opinion. Seriously, it's unacceptable. How can we, in 2022, let people live like this?"

Schilling has had enough. After eight years on Commercial, he's giving up his lease. "We've had it. It's finished for us," he told me. "We're gonna go. We're going to see where we're going to go. But, if it's possible, far away."

And that is the shame of San Francisco.

Roy Zeidan owns Discount Cigarettes, a small grocery store at Kearny and Commercial. He was there the morning the police found Messer. He's also fed up with City Hall.

"When (Mayor London Breed) got elected, she said she'd clean the city up," said Zeidan. "She did nothing. You call 311 (a city program that provides street cleaning and homeless services) and they send someone in two or three hours. Maybe the next day. We call the police, they do nothing.

"It should be the most beautiful city in the world. But it's disgusting."

It's hard to walk our streets and hear the despair. I talk to cops, shopkeepers, bartenders, homeless and more. They all share the same sense of hopelessness. We see the problems all around us. We hear our neighbors crying out for help. But nothing gets done. Nothing changes.

When the history is written, years from now, we will be judged harshly for standing by helplessly while our fellow man wallowed in the depths of addiction and mental distress. For allowing hard-working merchants to fail as a result of dirty streets and filthy conditions. They'll judge us for a shocking inability to maintain order and provide compassionate care.

They'll judge us for ignoring Sean Messer's cry for help. And that is our shame to bear … collectively.

COMMERCIAL STREET SAN FRANCISCO, CA

IMG 6546. Commercial Street, San Francisco where Sean Messer was found dead on the morning of August 10, 2022
Al Saracevic/The Examiner

Sean Messer, 42, was found dead in the corner of this parklet in front of City View Restaurant on San Francisco's Commercial St. on Aug. 10, 2022
Al Saracevic/The Examiner

Case#: 2022-0964
Cause and Manner of Death Report
CITY AND COUNTY OF SAN FRANCISCO
OFFICE OF THE CHIEF MEDICAL EXAMINER

DECEDENT INFORMATION

Decedent Name: **MESSER, SEAN**

Alias Name(s): DOE_2022_177

Date of Death: 08/10/2022

AGE: 42

Examination Type: AUTOPSY

Pathologist: Ellen Moffatt MD

Manner of Death: Accident
Method of Death: D...

Manner of Death: Accident
Method of Death: Drug-related

ACUTE MIXED DRUG (FENTANYL, COCAINE AND METHAMPHETAMINE) INTOXICATION

ALPRATIOLAM bentiodiatiepine derived -

ALPRAZOLAM PRESENT

PROLOGUE

I never liked writing in first person as I am doing now. But I do so to echo the raucous crying out of a homeless, addicted, mentally ill man, Sean Messer. I am his aunt who tried to help him for decades but failed. Now in this writing, I yearn for his crying out to count for something.

Sean's cries, I now realize, were not his alone. His pain lingers on assaulting the minds and hearts of all who are capable of compassion. Profound blows have been dealt to those who knew and loved him most.

To me, Sean's story is a metaphor of sorts - representing the thoughts, feelings, and actions of so very many whose lives have been affected by lost loved ones living and dead. At times the narrator's "I's" may become "We's," because together our caring, trying, sadness, and repeated failures to help, often leave us feeling that every door is shut and the mountain too high to climb. It is to the wounded and to you who care that I dedicate this book.

As Sean's story unfolds, I invite you to come along and experience my face-to-face encounters with the man who taught me about homelessness, addiction, mental illness; and about how hope can connect with tragedy.

With the intimate detail that comes from Sean's and my face-to-face encounters, with excerpts from recorded conversions, with the wisdom of looking back on where things went wrong, and with the expert findings of neurobiologists and psychologists about trauma, drugs, and self-indent – we uncover hidden chapters of Sean's life.

The story is raving and educational. It promises to be a high-octane lib toward the kind of awareness that will fuel the desire for change.

Since Sean's death, I've been haunted by the futility of the status quo. Why is it that we cannot find a place for the homeless mentally ill to lay their heads? Why can we not begin at least with a model? The need for long-term treatment and safe community is strikingly apparent. Yet for decades little has changed.

It's hopeful and beautiful to know that the majority of Americans do care about the homeless, addicted, and mentally ill. We are of one caring mind. Across America multitudes work in food pantries, provide clothing and supplies, offer medical and counseling services, pray, make donations, organize web sites, film documentaries, speak on television, and shout out with newspaper articles. Americans reach out to the world. But these caring acts are like sparks in stubble and green shoots in a desert of systemic failure that has put off transformational change for decades. Until the scales of the status quo tip toward systemic and private sector creative change, the status quo will continue.

After decades of frustration and sadness about the daily inhumanity that plagues us, it occurred to me that we need to try something different, something new. So, I threw a dart and decided to do an experiment.

What if I raised my voice to grab the attention of someone who has already succeeded in bringing about change for the good of others?

Why not shout out to the *Change Makers?*

On my desk is a big brown envelope addressed to someone who:

I believe has the mind and heart to care about the those who have no voice, no power, and nowhere to lay their heads, the homeless mentally ill Is successful in working for the common good Has a voice of considerable influence. Knows how to get things done

Is widely known, networked, and connected (so if unable to engage in this need, will pass it on to another who may help)

Change Makers are all around. Heads of corporations, superstars of sports and the arts, media personalities, writers, heads of hospitals and universities, philanthropists, even politicians, if they're motivated to right a faltering moral compass. All are used to receiving big brown envelopes!

I invite you as you read on, to put your sight on a *Change Maker,* and later if you see fit, please join me in launching *The Strategy of the Big Brown Envelope.*

For now, I write and long for the day when the final stroke of ink rolls on to the last page of what has become a book.

I can see it now.

I slip the book into the envelope, drive to the Post Office, send it down the chute, and in my heart I whisper,

> "This one's for you, Sean, and for all whom you represent. Maybe we'll get lucky, and someone will pull branches from that systemic log jam so it can flow into something good."

To many this will seem like a "what the heck there's nothing to lose Hail Mary." And it will be. But to others, this secular act of mailing a book may become an internalized ritual honoring the life of Sean and others who have suffered his plight. Whichever, it'll be a day when we took action, and it's likely, we'll remember.

It's worth noting that we're wired for making benevolent change and for collaboration. Within, we have the right stuff.

From our earliest beginnings as species Homo Sapiens, our brains have been wired to collaborate for survival. Over thousands of years of migration, molecules wrapped deep in our DNA moved us through an Ice Age to France where we painted cave walls with symbolic art. Never could these physical, neurological and cultural leaps in our history have taken place without our minds compelling us to collaborate. Together we learned to adapt to harsh climates by developing tools for the hunt and for tanning hides. We fashioned bone needles to sew warm clothing, and we made bone hooks for fishing. We even perforated shells for necklaces that signaled social roles and identity. Visionaries and our own experience tell us that

> "As the mind goes, so goes the heart.
> As the heart goes, so goes the mind."
>
> Michael A. Singer, *The Untethered Soul*

For us, collaboration and caring are the fuel for invention, innovation, mindsets, progress, and change. Simply put, "The We" within, is the exact right stuff for the kind of Crying Out that can affect change. Together we can amplify Sean's voice and send it out into the minds of others. How motivating it is to know that every successful invention or movement designed to improve the lives of others began with a single voice that became the voice of the many.

There's more good news. Psychologists tell us that beneficial to our welfare, buried deep in our psyches, is a longing to belong to something bigger than ourselves - to something greater than just oneself alone. We probably don't think of it this way, but the desire to band together with others to bring about change for the good of the homeless mentally ill is an example of being part of a collective consciousness.

"Collective consciousness is a unitary, collective, overarching, inclusive mind made up of individual minds, that when connected and bonded, become a spiritual energy that exists for the good of others. It's a force bigger and more powerful than that of each mind standing alone...

"Individual minds are like the many drops in an ocean. Together they are one thing, the ocean..."

"*Why Does Collective Consciousness MaAer?* "Identifying ``with the highest forms of human consciousness can clear our vision, prevent the hardening of our moral and ethical arteries, and inspire us to action. These are not ordinary times. Boldness is required – including boldness about how we think about who we are, our origins, our destiny, and what we are capable of. I do not think of ONE MIND as a philosophical play thing. It is not a luxury concept to be contemplated at leisure. Urgency is afoot!"

Larry Dossey, M.D., *New York Times* Best Selling Author. *One Mind – How Our Individual Mind Is Part of a Greater Consciousness and Why It Matters*

AUGUST 10, 2022

I was 3000 miles away, living in the Midwest when I received a call from the San Francisco Medical Examiner's Office. When the name came up, I knew something dire had happened. A moment later came a deep blow to the heart. Sean was dead. I knew the day would come, but I wasn't ready. We hadn't gone to where we needed to be. We hadn't gone anywhere.

I wandered for days and months, sunk in the sadness, frustration, and futility of Sean's life. It accompanied me everywhere – putting on my socks, driving the car, in the grocery store, when I cooked supper, and as I looked at the moon on dark nights. I couldn't shake the tragedy of how Sean went on day after day for two decades with no sure food, no place to go to the bathroom and wash, no clean clothes, with painful rosng teeth, no one to count on, and no place to lay his head even in the frigid Chicago winters where some of his story takes place.

I cannot expect you as a reader to feel the sting of the Coroner's call or to think of Sean when you're putting on your socks. I cannot bring you the movie that would stun your senses and emotions into emblazoned memories. I cannot draw you in with the written words of a great writer. I am not capable of any of this; but still, I have hope for change because of who I believe you to be. You are the ones who slip into other people's shoes, see the world that they see, and walk where they walk. The work of awareness is In you.

With this reading, I invite you to expand this gib to yet another level. Energize your knowing by summoning your imagination to take you to places you've never been, or to relive your own common experiences of frustration, confusion, sadness, and failures to fix. With your imagination you can bring yourself into the stories – into Sean's story. See yourself walking down the Financial District in San Francisco. Hear him cry out in raucous rage. As you walk on, perhaps you see that you're the first who notices him slumped over in the corner of the Parklet - lifeless, with a pipe in his hand. … If, in the course of your reading, you pause here and there to conjure up the images, you will make his story memorable and bring it into your heart.

WHO WAS SEAN MESSER?
The Family into Which He Was Born

Sean's mother, Kari, was the second youngest of six children. Her growing up included divorced parents, the loss of her family home, remarried parents, and a second-time divorced mother who took Kari's little sister and moved far away to find herself and survive.

In the years before Sean's birth, Kari hung out with a drug crowd, became addicted, and ran away from Chicago to Florida. There she met up with another addict, Ray, who later became Sean's father.

Prior to Sean's birth, one could safely say that our parents and we siblings were like rats leaping over the gunnels of a sinking ship.

I'm not saying that we were rats through and through, but we had something in common. Into a tumultuous sea we leapt, tracking one another, seeking land. A gib of fate would hurl us onto a desert island. Then for us, we would find joy in being alive and concoct ways to survive. We would huddle for warmth, carve fish hooks to procure food, and spark narrow twigs into fire. The love we already had for one another would grow and trump the dire challenges ahead. That gib of fate would bring us safety, comfort, and hope as we circled around a warm fire as did our ancestors those many millenniums ago.

But fate did not gib us. Life's twisting undertow spit us onto different islands. Each one, separated and alone, stumbled along with but a sliver of hope for a new beginning. But even alone, each survived, and Kari too began anew.

Her new life wrapped around a beautiful baby boy, Sean, born in Florida in 1980. Physically, he was born strong and healthy. Kari loved him with the deepest love of a mother, but her miserable life with Sean's addicted father broke her. She craved peace and a way to numb the pain of the chaos that surrounded her. Once again, she found calm and release in drugs. Months later, Kari and Ray split up and both fled. Sean's father vanished altogether and forever. Kari headed back to Chicago to rehabilitate. Three-year old Sean was left behind to live with Ray's parents.

Sean's grandparents loved him, but Sean later told me that they didn't protect him - likely from their lack of awareness that he was being sexually abused by relatives.

He went through life tormented subconsciously, and later, consciously by these immoral acts as they played out in his fragmented sense of self.

In raising him his grandmother also believed that a child's misbehaviors were caused by Satan within. Punishment and prayer were needed to drive out the devil. Sean told me about how as a little boy he was disciplined by his grandmother.

His thumbs were bound with string that was hoisted over the top of a door. He was told to raise his arms as the string was pulled tight over the door and fastened to the knob behind. He would stand like this with the string slicing into his thumbs while grandmother prayed, and until Sean promised, "Grandma, won't do it again, won't do it again."

Kari was in Chicago until Sean was about five years old. She was clean now, had a job and an apartment. A momentous day was about to take place. Sean's grandparents were bringing him to Chicago to reunite with his mother.

Summer, 1985 – The Day I First Met Sean

I first met Sean on the day the exchange took place at my house. He was the loveliest little boy ever, barely taking his eyes off his pretty mom. And very pretty she was with her curly blonde hair, tastefully done make up, and happy green eyes fixed on the new sunshine in her life. Sean took it all in loving being near her.

Sean with his Chicago aunt, Colleen, whom he had just met.

Sean was polite and accepting of all whom he had just met. I'll never forget him sitting on the piano bench with a wonderful family friend who accompanied him in singing, "Jesus Loves Me." His voice was gentle, clear, right on pitch. This was Sean - innocent, sweet, and shining bright with the goodness of a child. No one could ever have known what he'd been through.

In the afternoon we all went to a nearby beach, played in the water, sat on blankets and had snacks and drinks. I was sipping a can of beer when Sean's grandmother eyed me unapprovingly. "You shouldn't do that," she said. "Don't you know you're pouring the devil into your soul?" I was taken back, astounded at hearing such talk. I caught her face to see if she was joking. Then, without a word, I twisted the can into the sand and went into the water. I'd just learned first hand what Sean had been through, but for me, no punishment followed.

It's hard to imagine a child who from the beginning had been dealt so many low cards from the deck. By the time he was five, he'd been traumatized by multiple events. He experienced the raging outbursts of addicted parents that made him feel afraid and unprotected. He was sexually abused. And with drugs running the show, he was set aside, disregarded, and learned that he was unimportant.

And how can we even imagine his hurt and confusion when the mother who had suckled him, held him close, hugged, played with him, and slept nearby – walked out the door one day and was gone. His father too disappeared and never re-entered his life. And why, why, why, did it have to happen that this innocent little boy who believed that Santa drove a sleigh, also came to believe that the devil could be inside.

Sean: Neuroscience and Psychology

Neuroscientists and psychologists have studied trauma from every which way. They tell us that our subconscious minds are like an iceberg, and our conscious minds are but the tip. What sinks into our subconscious through experience drives behavior as it tells a story about who we are which in turn influences how we act and think.

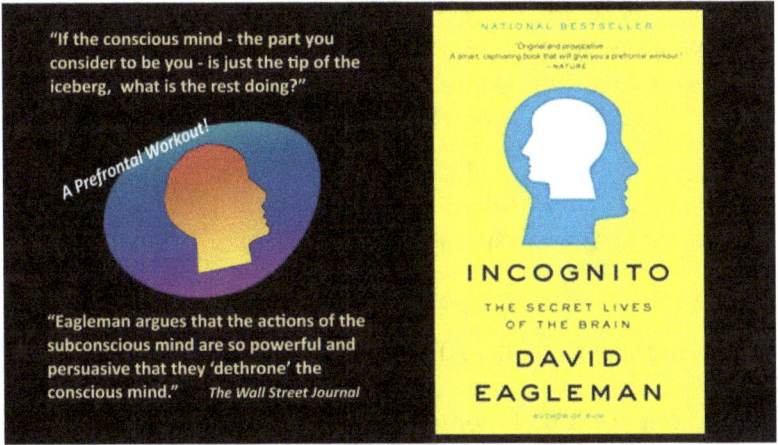

One of the most scholarly and highly regarded books on this subject was written by neuroscientist David Eagleman. He tells us that the subconscious mind is like a tape recorder that plays back experiences and long-term memories – over and over again in the subconscious. These taped messages are completely hidden from the conscious mind and become the "Johnny One Notes" of who we perceive ourselves to be. It does not play back in words or chapters.

It plays back in feelings about ourselves buried deep within. When the tape plays back traumatic experiences, the story becomes a dark fog hovering over one's sense of self. There is little doubt that young Sean navigated his world with angst, anxiety, uneasiness, unhappiness, foreboding... a festering caldron of negative feelings brought on by trauma. Feelings of which he was unaware.

As we go through life, the tape adds memories and experiences, but it does not revise or edit. Each new emotion-wrought experience whether nurturing or harmful attaches to the running tape. Simplified a billion times, we could say that what brings fear, hurt or demeans sticks. What nurtures and affirms sticks. What sticks deepest is determined by the intensity and kind of emotion that accompanies the experience.

Rock artist Pink Floyd sings about the angst of negative self- perception in his 70's hit album, *Brain Damaged*.

No longer can I remember exact words, but I do remember key themes that ran through his amazingly insightful music:

> There's a Dark Moon on the Grass
> A Lunatic Too
> There's Someone in My Head
> I Don't Know Who
> Lock the Door and Throw Away the Key
> There's Someone in My Head
> Please, Please, Please... Don't Let It Be Me

Thinking about the traumatic experiences lingering deep in Sean's subconscious by the Time he was five, it's easy to see that without serious psychological intervention and a new safe environment, he would be headed for hard Times.

Neuroscientist, Bruce Lipton in The Biology of Belief establishes that our minds have the ability to reset the negative self-perceptions of the subconscious. Through targeted therapies that bring hidden and negative experiences into the conscious mind, over Time, they can be worked on, overridden, and replaced with new perceptions, understanding, and positive actions.

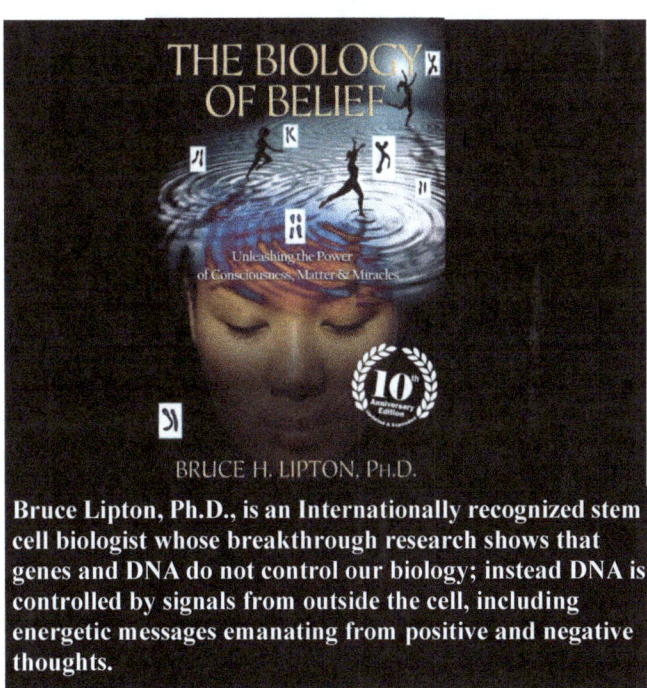

Bruce Lipton, Ph.D., is an Internationally recognized stem cell biologist whose breakthrough research shows that genes and DNA do not control our biology; instead DNA is controlled by signals from outside the cell, including energetic messages emanating from positive and negative thoughts.

Note the subtle, Unleashing the Power of Consciousness, Matter, & Miracles.

Matter = the molecular level of brain cells that set into motion the synapse responses to environmental signals (therapies and safe environment).

Miracle = we build new pathways/networking in the brain.

But for Sean no intervention came. He was just a little boy suspended on the dark side of the moon with no light in sight.

COLLATERAL DAMAGE

Yet, in spite of all this, for Sean, just being with his mom brought light into his life. He also had a new loving Chicago grandmother, an aunt who would hammer nails with him to build a bird house, and he went to an award-winning school that had a visionary principal and supportive teachers. But even with repeated efforts, Kari could not break from the drugs. Day by day, that sinister marauder lurked. With each pill, needle, smoke - her addiction suffocated her will and yanked at her brain tissue re-arranging its architecture.

Gone was the job, the apartment, the award-winning school. In came a new charming but drug afflicted husband, and a gypsy's life moving from place to place. Kari, Sean, and the new husband were adrift, with phone and address unknown.

Gone too, was the safety net that Sean's Chicago grandmother gave him. With her living nearby he could call at night if his mother hadn't come home. Or she would console him when he told her about being afraid when he was left in the car to sleep while his mom connected at the bar in the bowling alley. Grandma would care for him and wrap him in her arms. And she tried with all her mother's love (at Times tough love) to help Kari straighten out.

But the marauder was ever present spreading its foul breath over three lives. All the while, in many ways, Sean was collateral damage.

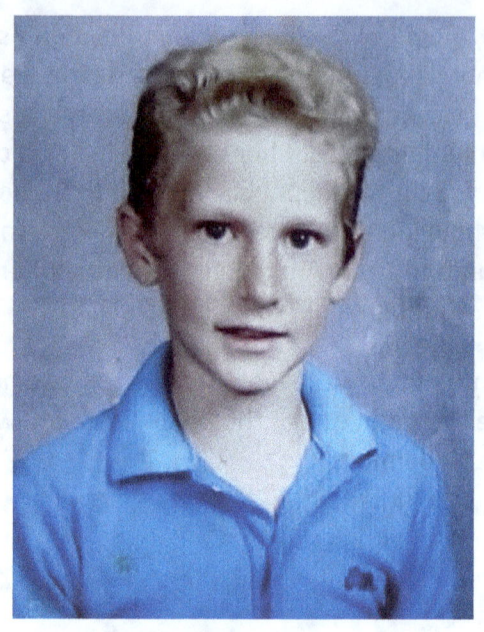

Sean was nine years old when he sustained yet another loss. Not only had his safety net grandma become separated from him by distance, but she suffered a severe stroke that left her unable to read, write, walk, or talk. That someday dream of his of when they would reunite, would never come. The safety and love he once counted on was gone.

The new kind of relationship that would have evolved with sweet Sean reaching out and his impaired grandmother responding with joy and love would never come to be because there was a turning point.

SPRING, 1989: TURNING POINT THIRTY MINUTES to LIFELONG REGRET

One Sunday in May my brother and I were working feverishly building a wheel chair ramp so mom could be at my house on weekends. During the work week she had 24-hour care so she could be at her own home that she loved. But she looked forward to weekends to be with my family, the dog, great food, and the Cubs on T.V. Through her indomitable spirit and extensive therapy, she was now able to move in a wheel chair, use one arm, and though she never regained her speech, she communicated brightly with sounds and inflection.

Before we finished putting the railings on the ramp, I ran over to mom's place to see if she had awakened from her nap. When I got there a car drove up. Out of the blue, and after all these months, Kari had come to visit.

We went in the house and checked on mom who was still dozing. She looked so frail and small, diminished, curled up in the blanket. I knew it hit Kari too. I wanted to say, "See, all these months she's needed your love and support too...," but I held back.

We moved to the living room where we stood about six feet apart, small talking. Kari looked Tired and worn like a young woman run down by a lot of hard miles. There was no sparkle, no warmth, no how's mom been doing. She seemed flustered to see me.

The conversation was strained, each of us searching for something, anything to say. We never sat down like people do when they visit. We just stood there like two people wanting to leave.

I started telling her about the ramp we were building and asked if she would stay and fix lunch for mom when she woke up. I needed to get back to help set up the railings.

I barely finished talking when she welled up ready to cry. Then her face turned steely and angry.

"I can't stay here," she blurted, "I've got things to do."... She accelerated. "Yeah, yeah, you!... You've got the whole ball of wax and I'm sick of it. Always the big deal - in charge of everything! I'm gonna smack you down! I'm gonna smack you hard!" She clenched her hand making a fist, holding it tight and still – elbow near her mid-section flexed to strike. Then raising her arm, she took a brisk step toward me.

She was out of control, but I was incensed with a cascade of emotion of my own about how much I had sacrificed, given up my life as I had known it to care for mom. My own anger seething, I did not draw back.

Intense and firm, I took one deliberate, very slow step toward her. Looking her in the eye, I leaned in... and said forcefully, separating each word from the next, "I don't think you want to try that." She seemed stunned by my demeanor, paused, and faded back.

Turning away toward the door, she started crying. Under her breath she muttered, "Damn it. Damn it, I wish I never came here."

In the past she avoided me when she could, but now It was crystal clear that she wanted me out of her life altogether - to butt out, to leave her alone so that I wouldn't find out what I already knew - that she was addicted.

Out she went, the door banging shut. As she drove away, I thought. Buh out? I'll be glad to. No more drama, no more chaos, no more calls about money, no more aggravating dead ends to endure. Thanks for slamming the door.

At first, I was proud of myself for standing up to her - patting myself on the back for confronting a bully, feeling righteous that I had done something kind of brave.

It wasn't 'til many years later that I realized that it was this thirty minutes in May that was the turning point for losing my connections with Sean. When Kari went out the door, he went too. Sean's and my space together disappeared. For us there would be no more birdhouses to build.

And I'm the one who made that happen.

TURNING POINTS: REDEMPTION AND THE WISDOM OF LOOKING BACK

How could one small step in the wrong direction, a moment of "leaning in," lead to so much abandonment and pain for both Sean and Kari? How could one fleeting interaction make a bad thing far worse than when it started out?

When involved in confrontations involving addiction, how much can we blame ourselves for not taking positive action when we're not equipped to understand the need and have not developed the ability to turn things around?

Our redemption lies in the fact that we would have acted differently if we understood the need and knew how to generate a saving outcome.

There are lessons to be learned through the wisdom of looking back that we can bring into the present. I've come to believe that when our unbridled emotions and self-centeredness become flight or fight knee-jerk reactions, we're headed full speed for the edge of a cliff. In these destructive moments with Kari there was something I needed that I did not have. How could I have turned the car around? All these years later, I now know what was missing - knowledge of the biochemistry of addiction, and a cultivated disposition of compassionate caring.

From Mind to Heart

"Your Perspective is always limited

by how much you know.

Expand your knowledge,

and you will transform your mind."

Bruce Lipton, Ph.D. *The Biology of Belief - Unleashing the Power of Consciousness, MaAer & Miracles.*

"As the mind goes,

So goes the heart.

As the heart goes,

So goes the mind."

Michael A. Singer, *The Untethered Soul.*

COMPASSIONATE CARING

Cultivating a disposition of compassionate caring flows from knowledge. Something I needed to know back then when dealing with Kari was what modern science has discovered and recognizes as the starting point for therapeutic rehabilitation.

What if I had known that addiction is not a choice that anyone makes. It's not a moral failure. It's not an ethical lapse. It's not a weakness of character. It's not a failure of will. **What it actually is, is a response to human suffering. It is an attempt to escape pain and suffering – to get relief - temporarily... AddicQon is not the prime root of the problem of addiction - the pain is.**

What Kari needed from me was not judgment that she was a bully and wanted me out of her life. What if I had understood that her actions were straight forward screams of unresolved pain. **Addiction is all about trauma.**

Content from *Ted Talk*: *The Best Science Based Explanation of Addiction*. Dr. Gabor Mate worked as Medical Coordinator of the Palliative Care Unit at Vancouver Hospital. His long-term research and practice has been dedicated to parents challenged by hard core addiction, mental illness, and related conditions.

In that thirty minutes of regret I didn't realize that I was fueled by popular, misguided notions about addiction itself. During the confrontation with Kari, she wasn't seen by me as worthy of respect. I hadn't the least inkling that she was vulnerable, wounded by trauma like Sean, and in serious, unrelenting pain.

It's redeeming to recognize that the knowledge about addiction that could have served as a catalyst for changing the course of my speeding car was but an early dawning light in the eyes of the scientists themselves.

The explosion of research, advanced imaging technologies, and the ubiquitous handing off of computers, cell phones, and the Internet to the general public was just beginning. Today, however, knowledge is but a click away, and it's our responsibility to tend to it.

Until recently, I never realized that there was such a strong link between knowledge and cultivating a disposition of compassionate caring. Looking back gives us the opportunity to put the pieces together. Like well-oiled hinges on an easy swinging door, knowledge opens to new perspectives about addiction, which by some benevolent act of nature, become the necessary catalyst for compassionate caring. One side is facts, the other poetry; one side is mind, the other heart. Working in tandem, the two carry us across thresholds that lead to stepping back instead of leaning in, of listening instead of talking-over, of reaching out a hand instead of making a fist.

A MOTHER'S LOVE
SEAN AND THE MERCY HOME
FOR BOYS AND GIRLS

Years passed. We siblings saw little of each other, though there was an occasional grapevine. The word was that with Kari and Sean not much had changed - drugs and instability continued.

The part I knew about happened in mid-winter 1993. Kari called humbling herself asking for money because their heat was to be turned off. By this Time, I'd softened, and in my regret about the past I was relieved to help out.

I thought we'd broken through in our relationship, but there were no more calls - just months and months of silence. I worried that something dire had happened and tried to track them down. Everything was a dead end until I found the phone number of their land lady. All I wanted to know was if she'd seen them and if they were O.K..

After I introduced myself and told the lady that I was Kari's out of town sister, she erupted, spewing out every detail of the misery they had caused her and her family. She was trying to get them evicted for not paying rent, but it was taking forever. There were strangers coming in and out of the apartment at all hours of the night. There was drug paraphernalia strewn about the property.

Her little granddaughter found a needle while playing in the backyard. She unloaded, I'm sure thinking that I was part of it, but I managed to apologize, calm her down, and told her I'd try to help. But there was a problem; Kari, Sean, and the new husband were on the run, and once again address and phone were unknown unknown.

Again, a few years passed with the grapevine speaking of sightings here and there.

Then big news came, the semblance of a miracle. Kari placed Sean in The Mercy Home for Boys and Girls. He was fibeen, ready for high school.

At rock bottom in her lowest depths, it must have been that Kari reached deep into the implanted spirit of a mother's love. She realized that the only way she could save Sean from this life of misery was to release him, to let him go, to cut their ties so he could have a better life. In the midst of all the depravity, she gave Sean the greatest love of a mother.

Cutting ties with the one she loved most unconditionally was an ultimate sacrifice. They had strong bonds. All through life and without waver each of them referred to the other as "the sunshine in my life."

Even though Kari introduced Sean to pot when he was 12, he never blamed her for opening that door. When he told me about this years later, there was a light in his eyes. The memory of them getting high together was a sweet memory of bonding.

There they were, Kari and Sean against the world - laughing and mellowing out together as thick as Bonnie and Clyde reveling in those moments of skirting the law.

If you had to pick from a hundred of the best places to rescue a young man in crisis, Mercy Home for Boys and Girls would top the list. Mercy Home is a full-time residential treatment program sponsored by the Catholic Archdiocese of Chicago. It serves youth suffering from trauma and crisis. It's an open campus that provides health care, meals, and residential care 365 days a year. Participation in programs is completely voluntary. Kari would retain legal guardianship. All Sean had to do was to commit to changing his life by taking part in programs designed to stabilize, rehabilitate, and open doors to a successful life.

Once admired, residents give back by organizing and participating in service projects that benefit the elderly, veterans, children with disabilities, victims of natural disasters, and more.

While the boys benefit from adhering to the structure that is built into their daily schedules, they travel to school, work after-school and summer jobs, visit friends, take walks, play sports, participate in extra-curricular activities at their schools and back at the Home, and more. In short, they live their lives as typical teens. (See Website: Mercy Home for Girls and Boys).

For the first time in his life, Sean was living in a safe haven free of chaos and danger. He had a new life surrounded by new friends and professionally trained, warm, caring adults.

Though the Home was open for visitations from family, Sean missed his mother deeply and longed to be with her, but she convinced him to stick it out. She promised she would rehab, and that soon they would be together again.

Sean thrived at Mercy Home, graduated, and through Mercy Home Job Services was hired by a prestigious Downtown Chicago Law Firm not far from his Mercy Home base. This was ideal since as a graduate from Mercy Home he was able to take part in the Mercy Home Community Care Programs.

Community Care invites all former residents to participate in programs that offer ongoing support, encouragement, and resources. It ensures that those who have transitioned from residential programs can always rely on their extended Mercy Home family to help them succeed far into the future. Sean could receive counseling, attend seminars and social events, and be connected by Mercy Home with resources throughout the community.

At the law firm Sean worked in the mail room and delivered mail to the offices. He had a friendly personality and some of the lawyers began calling him by name. He was learning about the polite camaraderie that was part of the professional world.

Smart, energetic and personable, and after a few years of proving himself, Sean's duties increased. He was now trusted to deliver documents to the Cook County Court House. Life was trending upward. He now had his own cubicle, desk, computer, phone, salary, and an apartment with a roommate.

A BREAKTHROUGH

What had been lost was found. After years of not knowing Kari's whereabouts, she called, this time not asking for money, but asking for help. I broke the ice by telling her that I heard that she'd done a wonderful thing for Sean. I already knew he was thriving, but I had her tell it. She was bursting with pride about all he'd accomplished, then she transitioned. "I can't let him know about me. I'm not doing so good. I need help." She broke down sobbing.

She must have been desperate; after all, this was the person who wanted to smack me in the face. But the conversation flowed. I felt privileged that she was opening up to me. I remember the exact words I said to her, "Kari, I'm going to get behind you on this. I'll give it what I got. Let's figure out what we're going to do."

There and then we started to make a plan. She was without money or transportation, was off on her own sleeping in a basement by the furnace at a friend's house.

We went through the logistics. I'd do the research, make the calls, and get something plugged in. She liked the idea of starting with an advocate and a counselor. We figured that down the line they would hand off to a program.

I started right away the next day and hit gold. I reached a great counselor who was experienced and compassionate. She had a cancellation and was able to schedule an intake interview for Kari. Now all that was needed was to get Kari there. We were set. She was familiar with the location and a couple transfers on the busses was doable.

I strutted around airy over the great thing that was happening. On the day of the interview I watched the clock picturing them conversing. I saw Kari's pretty green eyes lit with attention and hope, and the kind face and encouraging words of this counselor pulling her in. This was the beginning that all of us siblings sitting on our deserted islands had hoped for - after all these years, Kari and Sean together were stepping toward happiness.

A few days went by, and I hadn't heard from Kari. I was burning with curiosity about how the meeting went, so I called the counselor. Finally getting through she answered, "I'm glad you called. Is Kari all right? She didn't show up..." I told her I didn't know what happened, I would get back to her. But I never did.

Thinking back, I now know what may have helped. Thinking comprehensively about the situation. I needed to ask myself every possible question about what could go wrong for an addicted woman who was dependent on drugs to relieve pain and knew she would have to give them up. Any escape route would seem better. What if I had showed up at the basement where she slept and took her to meet the counselor? I needed to attend to every detail but didn't. I lived hundreds of miles away, but had I known, I would have hit the road.

2008

THE UNTHINKABLE

"I'VE GOT SOME BAD NEWS"

It was my older brother on the phone. No "Hello," no nothing. He just came out with it. "I've got some bad news, Kari's dead!"

As I write this, I can barely find the words. I see myself standing in the kitchen holding the phone - feeling that instant plunge to the heart that yet stills me in the moment. I could not speak.

My brother continued, "She died in the hospital. It was an acute mixture of drugs. She was alive for a while, but they couldn't save her. She drifted away. The doctors said it was most likely accidental. ... The story is, she wasn't feeling good, had a bad cold or something, and took some drug to feel better. But she had a lot of methadone in her system too, and the mixture was deadly.

"God! She's 52 years old! Dead!"

"What about Sean?" I asked.

"Mercy Home is trying to reach him. They'll call back."

What was happening to Sean now was unthinkable. How is it possible that one person could be assaulted by so much pain and loss - over and over, year by year, layer by layer.

What could be running on that tape in his subconscious mind about who he perceived himself to be?

I hadn't seen Sean in years. I'll never forget when he walked into the funeral home. He was a man now, 28 years old. In he came wearing a black trench coat, with a sleek back pack slung over his shoulder. He was over 6 feet now and looked every inch of a Downtown Chicago young executive. At his side was Holly, his counselor from Mercy Home. It was clear that she'd been in his life and knew him well. She glanced over at him from Time to Time like a mother proud and protective of her son.

The family and guests were drawn to him, comforted him expressing sympathy and the desire to keep in touch. Throughout, he held it together, was gracious, and did not break down except for a moment during the Memorial Service that a musician friend and I had planned. The music was sacred and very moving. And when, during the eulogy, I spoke about the deep love that Sean and his mother shared, he teared up. Holly glanced at him sensing his pain.

When the wake ended, Kari's husband approached. Handsome in a blue suit and tie, he expressed warm thanks for the beautiful ceremony. He was smooth socially, and I could see how Kari was attracted to him. Without the drugs it seemed that they would have been great for one another.

His was a giving moment. Holding the container of Kari's ashes he said, "Jan, if you will, I'd like you to take these. I've been moving around. It would be good for Kari to have a home." I thanked him and felt honored, but mostly I was humbled considering the way I treated her in the past.

Right before we all left, Sean, Holly, and I stood talking. I showed Sean the container of ashes and told him that I would keep them for him until he was settled in his new life. "You and your mom should be together."

Holly gave me her card and invited me to call anytime to catch up on Sean. That was the door that opened for me to get back into Sean's life. I would run through it and burst in, but it wasn't so easy.

THE DREAM

During the writing of this section on Kari's passing, I pulled out memorable scenes from the past that took days to piece into her and Sean's story. It was mull over and mull over until it got on the page. Then once it did, the very next day something extraordinary happened.

Early in the morning before the sun rose I had a dream , to a messy incomprehensible one, but one that was lucid, clear, and well defined. It was a neurological event in the visual cortex of my brain that was protecting and refreshing itself by reassembling pieces. It was relieving me of the angst of Kari's tragedy and the gaping new wound that was Sean's. It was also signaling that it wasn't over, there was more to come.

In the dream Sean and I were in a large group and saw one another from a short distance. He was spit and polished; fresh haircut, shiny shoes, pressed dockers pants, and a collared tan textured long sleeve shirt that complemented his sandy brown hair. He looked tall, relaxed, like inside he was balanced and in harmony with himself. There was a calm aura about him. This young man had the world by the tail, anticipating the joy of where he would be going next.

I was there filled with joy and euphoria spontaneously ready to call out, "Sean, why don't you come home with me." But the dream ended abruptly before any words were spoken. I awoke in that dark morning reaching for pen and paper, wondering... wondering so deeply about what may have happened and what did.

THE CRASH

Going back to work after his mom's death wasn't easy for Sean. The burst of energy and status he felt before at work slipped away. Nobody knew what he and his mom had been through and how much they meant to each other. For so long a Time the two held on to one another staying afloat. Theirs wasn't an ordinary life, but it was filled with extraordinary bonds. His grief was unbearable, the pain impossible to escape.

Sean slacked off at work and started using his computer in ways inconsistent with company policy. One day he was caught with illicit nude pictures on his screen. Further investigation yielded more of the same along with searches unrelated to company business. It's probable too, that Sean was suspected of using drugs. He had transgressed policies of a prestigious law firm, and for Sean, there were no second chances. Termination followed.

Sean needed a job, and he needed one fast to keep up with the semblance of a normal life. But he would have no letters of recommendation coming from anywhere.

He knew some of the bike messengers who delivered to the firm, and quickly landed a job. It was common for messengers to come and go. Among them was a wild, unstable bunch known as the "Bike Peddlers," those who rode and sold to keep their drug habits going.

There was an adrenalin rush with the fast riding - zigzagging through Chicago's Downtown lanes, and it brought with it a good bit of camaraderie. Sean would fit right in.

Months ago at the wake, Holly had opened the door for me to stay in touch. That's when I promised myself that I would run through that open door and burst back into Sean's life.

So it was that Sean called. He needed a bike, and not just any bike. This one had to be for racing with a lot of gears, and special-order tires and compact handle bars to weave in and out of traffic. And could it be black?

Bike = job = $ = apartment and food. It was Time to toss a rope so Sean wouldn't teeter and crash.

That's what we do when someone needs help. The collaboration and caring springs from our ancient roots. Some call it enabling. But it's not so black and white. Who wouldn't throw a rope to one clinging to the edge of a precipice? And who would want to live with themselves if they didn't? The "I" in this story continues to be the "We."

And there are more complexities. The bike was more than a bike. It was the way Sean pedaled into a full-blown subculture of users infesting the messengers. There he went with his hair on fire speeding into an abyss that would relieve his pain - just for a little while...

Yes, running through that open door bursting back into Sean's life wasn't going to be easy - not easy at all.

The "I" is the "We."

Going back to work after his mom's death wasn't easy for Sean. The burst of energy and status he felt before at work slipped away. Nobody knew what he and his mom had been through and how much they meant to each other. For so long a time the two held on to one another staying afloat. Theirs wasn't an ordinary life, but it was filled with extraordinary bonds. His grief was unbearable, the pain impossible to escape.

Sean slacked off at work and started using his computer in ways inconsistent with company policy. One day he was caught with illicit nude pictures on his screen. Further investigation yielded more of the same along with searches unrelated to company business. It's probable too, that Sean was suspected of using drugs. He had transgressed policies of a prestigious law firm, and for Sean, there were no second chances. Termination followed.

Sean needed a job and he needed one fast to keep up with the semblance of a normal life. But he would have no letters of recommendation coming from anywhere.

He knew some of the bike messengers who delivered to the firm, and quickly landed a job. It was common for messengers to come and go. Among them was a wild, unstable bunch known as the "Bike Peddlers," those who rode and sold to keep their drug habits going.

There was an adrenalin rush with the fast riding – zigzagging through Chicago's Downtown lanes, and it brought with it a good bit of camaraderie. Sean would fit right in.

Months ago at the wake, Holly had opened the door for me to stay in touch. That's when I promised myself that I would run through that open door and burst back into Sean's life.

So it was that Sean called. He needed a bike, and not just any bike. This one had to be for racing with a lot of gears, and special order tires and compact handle bars to weave in and out of traffic. And could it be black?

Bike = job = $ = apartment and food. It was time to toss a rope so Sean wouldn't teeter and crash.

That's what we do when someone needs help. The collaboration and caring springs from our ancient roots. Some call it enabling. But it's not so black and white. Who wouldn't throw a rope to one clinging to the edge of a precipice? And who would want to live with themselves if they didn't? The "I" in this story continues to be the "We."

And there are more complexities. The bike was more than a bike. It was the way Sean pedaled into a full-blown subculture of users infesting the messengers. There he went with his hair on fire speeding into an abyss that would relieve his pain - just for a little while... Yes, running through that open door bursting back into Sean's life wasn't going to be easy - not easy at all.

The "I" is the "We."

When you're riding in the black hole of addiction, a crash is inevitable. Most of your money goes for drugs and alcohol. So it doesn't take long to lose your apartment and find yourself living on the back stoop of an expensive downtown hotel. There you will be relieved of your expensive bike, what money you have, and even your shoes. Then disoriented and shamed, you disappear. You find a piece of cardboard in a dumpster, and print "Please Help," so you can sit somewhere and panhandle. Desperate, Sean sat on the cold cement holding his sign begging for money. He needed a bus ticket to Florida where he would try to find his father.

Sean settled at his Florida grandparents' place for a few weeks, his father showing up here and there. The story goes that things were cordial at first. They spent some days talking and smoking some pot, but Sean's persistent questions about being abandoned and asking for help, turned things sour. Words were exchanged, and Sean's father left washing his hands of Sean. The gist of it was, "… lots of luck, you're old enough, get it together." And just like before, he was gone.

Sean's Florida grandmother didn't take to the conflict. Sean was a man now, and not getting along with her son, Ray, was a divider. Sean should pack up and get out. But he had no money and nowhere to go. He was homeless and floundering. With the loss of his mother and the face-to-face rejection by his father, he hit bottom. To make life bearable, mind-altering drugs seemed the only solution.

THE DEEP DIVE INTO DRUGS

Sean didn't know it, but each Time he introduced narcotics into his blood stream by snoring, smoking, ingesting, or injecting - he set loose an army of small molecules that altered consciousness, affected cognition, and steered his behavior.

How this actually happens in one's body is well known by medical scientists, but not by the general public. Yet, we need to know because knowledge about the biochemistry of mood-altering drugs may be one of the hardest hitting deterrents for drug use, especially when taught at an early age. It takes just a short dip into biochemistry to build understanding about the devastating effects of these dangerous drugs. Sean lacked this kind of scientific knowledge - as do most addicts today.

(The biological data that follows is derived from David Eagleman's book, *Incognito: The Secret Lives of the Brain.*)

Neuroscientists and biochemists assure us that once ingested, users become slave to the chemical molecules that comprise mood altering drugs.

"If we knew nothing else about neurobiology, the mere existence of narcotics would give us all the evidence we require to know that our behavior and psychology can be commandeered at the molecular level." (Eagleman)

A molecule is a group of atoms bonded together representing the smallest unit of a chemical compound that can take part in a chemical reaction.

The reaction happens because the plus and minus ratio inside the atoms that make up the molecules are imbalanced and thus produce an electrochemical charge that's essential for brain cells to synapse, connect with one another.

The molecules are the movers and shakers that form new neural pathways in the brain. Then Bingo! The ultra-powerful chemical elements found in narcotics specifically target the brain network that registers rewarding events.

In Narcos free brains, pleasurable events can be as small as enjoying an icy lemonade on a hot summer day, exchanging smiles with someone in the grocery store, or feeling good because you received a compliment or a good grade. And, of course, they include our evolutionary thrust to survive and thrive - the big things like mating, enjoying food and water, making practical daily decisions that move life forward, socializing, and all things related to growth and happiness.

By tying positive outcomes to feel-good behaviors, our natural neural circuitry, (the mesolimbic dopamine system), optimizes and strengthens these neural pathways. They make us feel good, so we repeat them. Our natural biology is a quick and efficient learner.

But it doesn't have a "Wanted Sign" to warn about dangerous interlopers who move in and commandeer our neural circuitry.

Without Sean's knowledge or permission, the cocaine and other opioids that he ingested raced through his bloodstream, arrived in his brain, and told it that the euphoria he was feeling was the absolute best thing that could ever be happening.

These tiny chemicals, one thousand Times smaller than the width of a human hair, gave him insatiable cravings, that if resisted, result in unbearable pain. This is now the only message that screams in his head. He has no idea that his ancient circuits have been hijacked.

What makes cocaine and opioids like fentanyl, so addictive is that the accidental shape of their molecules is a perfect match with the lock-and-key shape of the dopamine neurotransmitter that makes communication with another brain cell possible. Moving through a specific channel with the dopamine neurotransmitter, the drugs now have a free ride into the microscopic machinery of the brain's reward circuits. No stops, no detours, clear sailing ahead.

Then danger! - The molecules in fentanyl, for example, head for the central nervous system (CNS), and can easily cause overdose and death because they overwhelm the body's ability to process sensors normally. These molecules dull and silence the body's warning systems for breathing and heart rate. Emergency signals to regulate go unsent, and without medical intervention, death occurs.

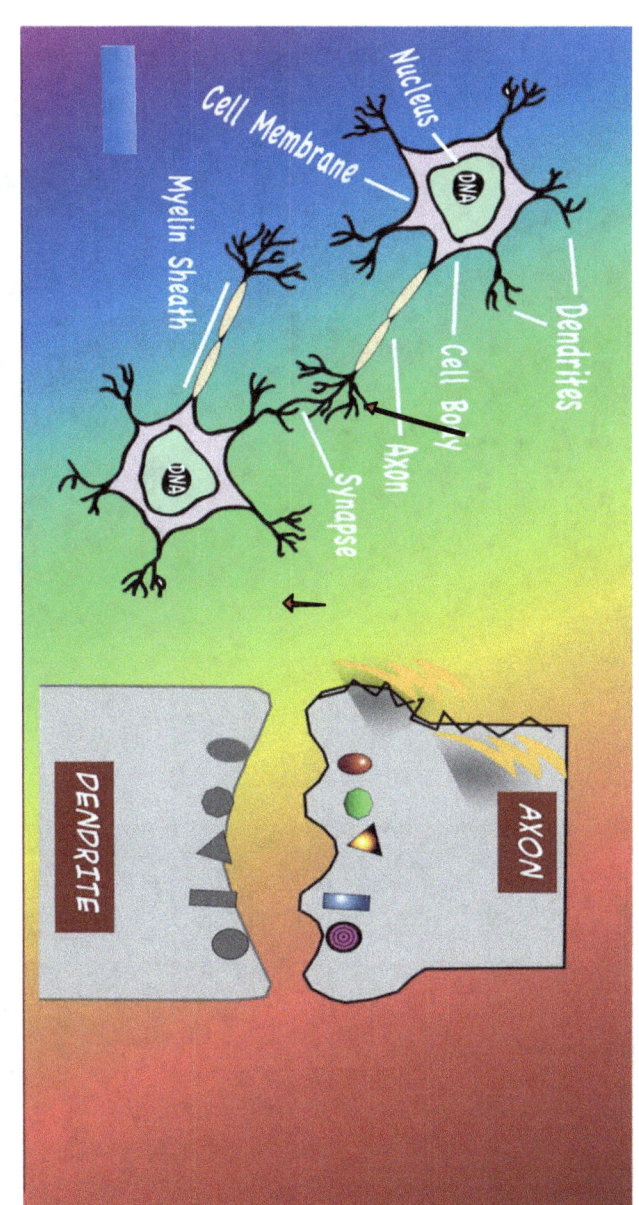

Note the artist's rendering showing the communication between two neurons happening at the synapse. The magnified image to the right illustrates the lock-and-key mechanism (triangle) that sends the dopamine and cocaine on its way to the brain's reward circuits - no stop signs, no detours, clear sailing ahead.

The brain runs the show

INCOGNITO

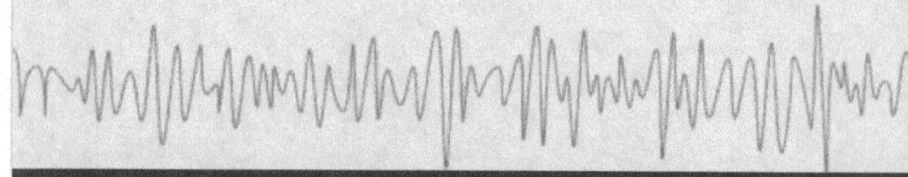

"Who you are depends on the sum total of
your neurobiology." And once that changes,
you are not the same person
that you once were.

David Eagleman, *Incognito:
The Secret Lives of the Brain.*

Sean believed he was rehabbing if he weened off hard drugs by swapping them for alcohol. What he didn't know was that the dopamine lock-and-key mechanism operates with a host of drugs of abuse: alcohol, nicotine, Psychostimulants, opiates, fentanyl, cocaine, morphine, amphetamines, and more.

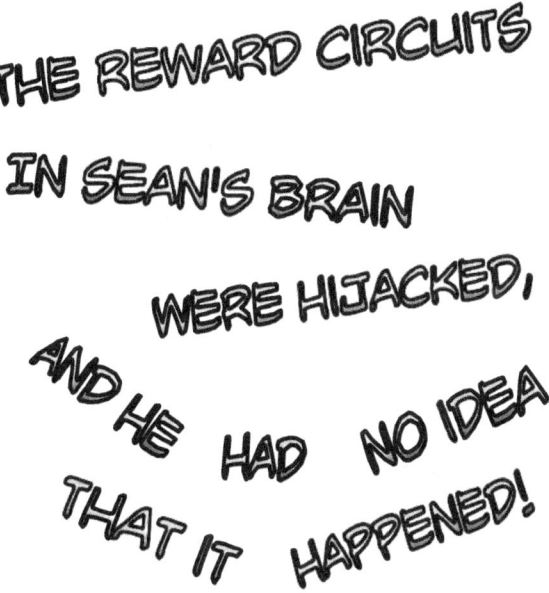

THE REWARD CIRCUITS IN SEAN'S BRAIN WERE HIJACKED, AND HE HAD NO IDEA THAT IT HAPPENED!

The architecture of Sean's brain had been rearranged and would no longer function normally. He was adrift, address unknown, staggering through life with a damaged brain.

"I'M IN TROUBLE. THEY'RE GOING TO SEND ME TO PRISON."

A year or so went by after Kari's death and there were no words or sightings of Sean. His mom was gone, Mercy Home was a thousand miles away, and he seemed tied to no one. From Time to Time I would worry about his whereabouts and even wonder if he was alive.

Then a call came from a County Jail in Florida.

"Auntie Jan, I'm in trouble. They're going to send me to prison." That was the message.

Apparently Sean had piled up a list of misdemeanors and felonies trying to survive on the streets with his damaged brain - vagrancy, possession of illegal drugs, pandering, trespassing on private property, disturbing the peace with threatening outbursts, and likely there was more. The urgency was to help.

I interceded by writing to the judge pleading for leniency because of Sean's traumatic past. I made innumerable calls to Sean's Public Defender who didn't call back until the eve of the trial. It was hopeless. In the judge's eyes Sean was a menacing addict and was sentenced to three years in a Florida County Prison.

During Sean's Time in prison our relationship grew. I wrote encouraging letters about how prison could help him turn his life around. He would be free of drugs when he got out.

I sent him bestselling self-help books, inspiring novels, art supplies (though very few were allowed since many had the potential for being used as weapons), and money for the commissary where he could buy clothes, snacks, stamps, writing paper, and more. He wrote back every month talking about the boredom of prison life, how he was staying out of trouble, how much he missed his mom, and he thanked me for the letters and money. He would do his Time and start a new life.

It was glaring to notice that never in the letters he wrote did he mention anything relating to the self-help books. Looking back, my hopes and expectations for Sean to come out of prison, get a job, and start a new normal life were unrealistic. He was still the same Sean walking around with unresolved trauma, and a damaged brain that no book could fix.

So far, the only plan he had was to have enough money in his account so that when released he could buy a bus Ticket back to Chicago.

NOT SO SWEET HOME CHICAGO

It was sweet for a while. Sean had Mercy Home, Holly, and me at a distance. But soon reality set in. Mercy Home Job Services were unable to help a man with a criminal record. Background checks were integral in the process.

Sean was unemployable, unable to rent a place to stay, and would continue to be homeless.

I researched help agencies and came upon a private citizen who started a non-profit business dedicated to helping reformed felons. I phoned him at Chicago's popular *Felony Franks,* a hot dog and sandwich shop west of Chicago's loop. He was a saint of a man who was once a felon and was instrumental in turning lives around through employment and fellowship in a supportive community of former offenders. The conversation was warm and hopeful. Sean should come by, and he'd see what he could do.

A door was open, but when Sean was a "No-show," it banged shut. Such was his ongoing pull into the murky bottom of a life dependent on drugs.

EVERY DOOR SHUT

Now that Sean was back in Chicago I was able to keep in touch with Holly and him from Time to Time. His needs were clear. First it was housing, but you can't get on a list for subsidized housing unless you can document income. I researched homeless shelters. He tried them but would never go back. The lights were on all night with people yelling. If you fell asleep you'd likely get robbed. Someone threw up on his shoes, and when he left, his clothes and belongings were full of bed bugs that were almost impossible to get rid of. Though not true, in his mind all shelters were like this. He would rather sleep on the street.

Sean could plug into counseling with Holly on a regular basis. She was professionally trained and an impressive advocate and practitioner. But he slacked off and often didn't show. Once again, addiction was the broker.

Drug and alcohol support groups were widely available. Sean attended a few Times but wouldn't continue. He considered it the same old "expletive!"

Finally we got Sean on a path designed to wean him off the more potent drugs. It took some doing, but I had liaisons - Holly and Rose, a dynamic personality-plus receptionist at a Methadone Clinic.

I set Sean up with a prepaid transportation pass so he could get to the clinic, food cards to fill in for the money he would have made panhandling and sponsored his sessions at the clinic. A bonus was that I could call Rose anytime to check on how Sean was doing and, if he was there, I could chat with him on the phone. Rose saw him every day and took him under her wing giving him common sense motherly advice about how to stand up and fly right.

Sean seemed steady for a while. He was showing up and getting drugs to lessen the pain of detox. The methadone doses were supposed to be lessened as the treatment went on. I needed to talk to the clinic's counselor to find out how far Sean had progressed. But the conversation was frustrating. According to the counselorr, Sean's doses had not been reduced at all because, "He has to want to get off the drugs, and he's not willing to go along with the program. It's all up to him."

I was astounded. Hadn't this counselor read books about addiction? He had a degree. Hadn't he learned about the kinds of therapies that are used in treating addicted parents? Who was running the show, Sean or him? The lack of progress had been the status quo for over a year now. It was fine with Sean's addicted brain, it was getting its daily fix.

How could it be that Sean was now addicted to methadone? Methadone - a substantial narcotic in the acute drug mix that took his mom's life! Something urgent needed to happen.

God bless Mercy Home. They held staff meetings about how to help Sean, and through their network they located a long-term residential rehabilitation program in Ohio. They had room for Sean if he would participate willingly and commit to the program's requirements. Mercy Home and I would be Sean's co-sponsors.

A week later Sean and I sat with Holly in her office at Mercy Home. She had arranged for Sean to come early to shower and dress in new clothes that Mercy provided. His street clothes were washed and in the dryer. He looked great, though he did show us his trembling hand indicating that he had missed his morning alcohol to rid the shakes. Other than that, he was aglow, happy to be with us. He seemed ready to hope.

Holly provided us with information on the program and had set up a phone conference with the Executive Director who was also a Pastor. Before proceeding, Holly slid the Commitment Document across the table to Sean. He read it carefully, then took the pen and signed. Holly and I eyed each other knowing that this could be the start of something big. Before leaving Sean was booked on a flight to Ohio. God bless Holly and Mercy Home!

A month went by. I called Holly to see if she'd heard any news about how Sean was doing. I thought he would have written by now, but neither of us had heard a thing. I called the Pastor Program Director. "… You're calling about Sean? Haven't you seen him? He up and left two weeks ago. He didn't take to the prayer and discipline… We gave him bus money and he took off for Chicago…"

COOK COUNTY JAIL, CHICAGO

Sean was laying low, probably ashamed that he was still addicted and didn't stick it out in Ohio. Almost a year went by. Then, a familiar call. This Time it was from Chicago's Cook County Jail.

"Auntie Jan, I don't wanna bother you, but … Can you help me get some stuff?" There was no explanation of why he was there, and I wasn't going to confront him. He was already upset and not making much sense. So there it went whipping through the cold Chicago wind - a rescue rope. In my mind he still needed to know that I was in his corner.

Weeks later I attended a conference in Downtown Chicago. Registering participants was Gloradina. She gave me a name tag and a lunch ticket, and with a beautiful welcoming face said, "Enjoy the day, Jan, we're glad you're here."

I told her I wouldn't need the meal ticket. At lunch I would skip out and visit my nephew who was nearby - at the Cook County Jail. "Drugs, drugs, drugs," I said flatly. I have no idea why this very private thought spilled out. I now feel that it was one of those strange synchronicities that happen between two people because somehow it was meant to be.

Though the line was bustling behind, Gloradina looked at me like we were the only two in the room. She handed me her card, and said, "Call me tomorrow. I may be able to help... Tomorrow," she said again. Then she was swallowed up by the crowd.

Going to Cook County Jail was a dangerous idea. I surely hadn't thought it through. Just because I was raised in the city didn't mean I was safe everywhere in the city.

The cab pulled up to a three-wide sprawling sidewalk in front of blocks of large buildings, some with bars on the windows. Before I stepped out, the driver asked if he should come back to pick me up. I got the impression he was looking out for me. Grateful, we set the Time and place.

I walked along the parked cars close to the street figuring that if I was approached I could run out in traffic and signal for help.

This was no place for a nicely dressed woman to be walking alone, and especially because it was obvious that she had no idea where she was going. Along the way, I tried a couple doors - locked and no one around.

From a distance I followed a group into an open foyer that was the registration area for jail visitation.

An officer at the counter looked at a data screen, "Sean Messer? This is General Population, Ma'am. He's down the block in Maximum Security."

"Maximum Security!" I hurried back past the parked cars, made no eye contact with passersby, and spent the next hour trying to get through security.

How naive I was to have my pockets full of everything a lady would need for a day-long conversation. Out it came into the bins, everything from the pockets, off with the coat, hat, shoes, socks, thumb through my hair, through the detectors, and, "Open your mouth, please." Then, "Have a seat Ma'am."

Finally I was cleared to enter a maze of narrow halls each separated by locked doors. The last locked door opened into a small room with two chairs and a glass window. From the moment I entered this building everything seemed dank and smudged. Here I was with Sean in his world that had run amok.

When he came in he looked down. His light was going out. "Hi, Auntie," he said sweetly. But when he talked he was in low gear. I listened and never did find out why he was in Max. I guess I didn't want to know. What good would it do?

The next day the sun came out. I contacted Gloradina. Turns out she was Chairwoman of the Board of Directors of a Family Treatment Center that serves "...the invisible, the ignored, the uninsured alcoholics and addicts of Chicago. No wonder she said she may be able to help. The Center is one of the nation's only outpatient treatment centers that offers individual counseling and educates about seven available core programs. Clients then may choose the kind of treatment they feel would be the best for their own journey to recovery. Rooting out and addressing trauma is the centerpiece of all the programs.

I visited the Center and met with Dave, the Center's Director. He was kind, ppersonable, and savvy about addiction from the street up to the halls of science. His passion about all the Center had to offer was contagious. It was easy to see that there were multiple ways for Sean to hook into the hope and get involved. Besides core programs corollary activities were offered - music, art, writing, poetry, roof parties for the eclipse, more; maybe there would even be a way for Sean to learn to play the guitar! The staff at the Center was highly trained and creative.

Sean was to be released from Maximum Security in two weeks. Apparently, he was arrested for disorderly conduct by exhibiting violent outbursts that could be a danger to self or others. In Maximum Security he would be given anti- anxiety drugs and when stable he would be released.

Contacting Sean through the Meth Clinic, it wasn't hard to sell him on the idea of getting help from the Family Treatment Center. "This is tailor made for you, Sean." I told him all about it, and about how he would meet new friends there too.

We set up a date to meet at the Center. When Gloradina said she'd be there too, I was ecstatic. Sean and I were finally going to pull a lever and hit the jack pot. Gloradina would be there! This was the gibed woman who made everyone feel important, and by her gib of nature pulled people in with her warmth and grace. Sean would love her.

Here we would be: Gloradina, Dave, and I pulling Sean from the black hole into a foxhole where elbow to elbow we had each other's backs. Along the way I learned that the four of us shared common bonds having been wounded by addiction in our individual lives. How beautiful it was going to be working together trying to defy gravity.

The three of us were at the Center at 10:00 as planned. I knew Sean was clear on the date and Time. He had a transit pass to ride to a nearby "L" station and would only have to walk two blocks to get to the Center. Over and over Gloradina and I looked out the windows, then down the street hoping to see him, but the minutes of waiting turned into hours. It was clear he wasn't coming...

A CRACK IN THE SIDEWALK

It's not easy talking to yourself when you're flat on your face with your nose in the dirt. You want to say, "Give it up, it's a lost cause, forget about the whole thing." But the dirt won't let the words come out. The only voice you hear is the one that haunts from your ancient roots.

"For your own survival and for his, you must keep going. Find the narrow patch of green that will take you through the Ice Age."

So I lifted my face, brushed the dirt from my eyes, and saw a sturdy, young, green shoot poking its head through a crack in a nearby sidewalk. Coming from this shoot of green, was a whisper, "Keep going."

So it was that on a brisk Sunday morning I sat in a church listening to a sermon. I didn't know the priest or anyone there, but it felt good to be passive and to be surrounded by all kinds of prayers going on. This particular priest had something to say, and to me, he was on target. Then and there I decided to talk to him about Sean. At the end of Mass I approached asking him if there was a Time when we could talk. He plugged me in for Saturday 3:00 confessions. They'd take place face to face in a small conference room. He didn't know it, but this talk wasn't going to have a thing to do with confession. I was going to catch his ear to create a haunting.

My thought was that if I clued him in about Sean's story and about how every effort to get help dead-ended, that he would come up with something to help Sean cross a threshold. I would explain that Sean's problems were so deep and incapacitating that even when a door opened, he was incapable of stepping through. He was like the paralyzed man in ancient Jerusalem who was unable to reach the healing pool because there was no one to carry him into the water. This priest, I reasoned, was connected all the way up to the Pope in Rome, while Sean and I were connected to no one who had the stretcher of a First Responder. We were the ones who would call up and say, "Hello, may we introduce ourselves? Our names are Nobody!"

Or maybe I would just say, "Father, how can I get help for someone who is so handicapped that he can't help himself?" Whatever I was going to say, I wanted it to stick in his mind big Time, and not be gone when I left. I would give him my phone number and hope to hear from him.

At three o'clock I arrived at the Church and saw Father in a front pew mediating. I slipped in about ten pews back so as not to disturb. No one else was there. For about twenty minutes I rehearsed what I was going to say, then wondered if he had forgotten about our appointment. I walked up to the pew where he was sitting and sat on the end. He didn't notice. Finally, I slid over toward him, stood up, and asked about our appointment.

In the confessional room, we sat down. I thanked him for his time, then from nowhere I blurted out, "Father, I didn't come here to confess, I came here to create a haunting!

His body pushed back in the chair. His face puzzled, and his eyes showed a slight tinge of fear. Instantly, I realized that I had scared him. "Who is this crazy person and what is she up to?" Immediately I toned down the bold demeanor and started telling him Sean's story, especially about how much I needed to get help for him. He listened compassionately, and talked about Charitable Agencies, (which I had previously visited). All in all, he tried, but there was no breakthrough but to pray.

Riding in the car on the way home I finally faced it. This was a last ditch effort, and it too, had failed. I'd imposed on this holy man whose whole life was dedicated to helping others. Did I really expect him to perform a miracle and carry Sean down into the healing pool? Turns out, our talk was useful. He gave me clarity about the cold, hard fact that the help Sean needed didn't exist. Where was the long-term treatment center where a poor, homeless, addicted, mentally ill man could lay his head?

Nowhere. Unless, of course, if you were rich - very, very rich.

Yet, there was something else to do. I still held the image of that sturdy, young, green shoot poking its head through the crack in the sidewalk. So far nobody had trampled it. The ancient voice crescendoed a significant memory.

When talking with Dave, the Director at the Family Treatment Center, he said something profound. "Jan, Sometimes the only thing left to do is to let them know that you love them." This would now be the little stretch of green that Sean and I would follow as we made our way through the Ice Age.

2017

UP CLOSE, FACE TO FACE WITH SEAN MESSER

In 2017 Sean and I began meeting in a Ride and Park Chicago Transit lot. He would take the Blue Line "L" and spot me waiting in the lot. I would see him quick stepping out of the station in his stained khaki pants, jacket, back pack, and Sometimes carrying a paper bag with a six pack to get him through the morning. My car was our clubhouse, his safe-house where he could talk freely and be out of the rain. At Times the conversions were flowing, lucid and even sweet, but just as quickly he could flash into diatribes about the injustice, abuse, and the disrespect he felt - every word of it jolting, but true and unexaggerated.

Overall, my role was straight forward, "Jan, sometimes the only thing left to do is to let them know that you love them." To me this meant that I would keep doing things to make his life easier, and it also meant that I would try to bolster his spirit. Throughout, I spoke my truth about how he was courageous, brave, resilient, and long suffering. But it was also clear that he was fragile. During each meeting I needed to encourage and not set him off.

Each careful word that I spoke felt like a step on thin ice.

One thing I knew for sure was that he needed to express himself. We talked about dabbling in the arts to get release. He jumped on this idea. He told me that he spent good Times at the Chicago Public Library. They had these pianos in rooms where you could play if you reserved them, and even get lessons. They had drawing books, and computers to use.

There we were looking out the windows of our clubhouse scoping out something good that could happen next.

But, at Times, our planning derailed.

One brisk morning in the Lot, Sean and I sat talking and I asked him about how he gets food and finds a place to sleep. He was in mid-sentence when his demeanor switched instantly. He stared out the passenger side window at a maintenance man picking up litter near a trash can.

"Do you see that guy? Do you see 'em? He's F****** with me. He knows who I am. I'm going to punch his face in. ... He's messin' with me!" Sean was seething, exploding before my eyes.

He reached for the door handle to burst out of the car, but he was unfamiliar with the button to release the lock. I grabbed onto the top of his left thigh, "Sean, Sean, don't do that. If you get in trouble, I will too. We got liquor in the car!" Thinking about it later, it seemed like he stopped because of some built in subconscious male desire to protect. It surely didn't seem like he had thought this through and controlled his rage. It was something else. He wasn't going to get Auntie Jan in trouble. He turned his head and stared straight out, fixed on the front window. I started to tell him that I thought the guy was just picking up butts, but he broke in sternly, "Quiet! ... Shhhh ... Shhhh" ... Leaning forward toward the windshield, his torso stiffened. "Listen. Can you hear 'em? ... Shhhh!"

He stared hard at the glass, his face carved in stone, set and still. There was no peripheral vision, no awareness of me sitting next to him. He was in a trance.

It hit me that Sean was in an altered state. I was afraid. Would he hallucinate that I was someone else, and rage because I was out to get him? There were no boxes to check in this situation. I slowly slid my arm to the left and put my finger on the unlocked button. I would press it to open an escape route in case Sean became violent. But would the click bring his attention to me? I took a deep breath and clicked. He remained fixed on the windshield. Next I slowly pushed the door ajar just enough to butt it open for a quick bail out. He stayed in the trance for about another minute with me sweating out every second. Then he sat back and rubbed his eyes. "I don't know, Auntie Jan, sometimes I get so frick'n mad. It eats me up ... You want one of these?" He offered me a beer. I was tempted to take one - to bond, but said, "No, thanks. You keep it. You might need it later." He was his sweet self again. We talked a little more about nothing much, then he thanked me for the food cards, picked up his brown bag, and faded into the crowd entering the station. I couldn't believe it; he had a bounce in his step like nothing had happened.

It later became clear that I had witnessed a psychotic episode that included antisocial behavior that could have become violent, as well as paranoia, hallucination, voices, and trance. All of it stuffed into an hour of a ticking Time bomb. Sean was mentally ill brought on by long term drug use. The use of methamphetamine alone can lead to paranoia, persecution delusions, and auditory and visual hallucinations. But Sean's long history of drugs also included cocaine, cannabis/pot, and alcohol - all mentioned in the scientific literature as inducers of psychosis.

What was obvious back then was that Sean was mentally ill and could be triggered into paranoia and delusion by his own fleeting glance beaming on some person doing almost anything. It could be that he saw someone talking about him, looking at him suspiciously, mocking him, planning an attack, agitating. All of this perceived aggression leaked into our conversations at one Time or another. Strangers were a problem.

"THEY SET ME ON FIRE!"

This is why, a few months later, when we were sitting in the car at the Lot, I dismissed something he was telling me. I'd been chattering about how he could take a class at the Art Institute, when he butted in and unloaded on me. "Jan, you don't understand anything! You live in La-la-land. Get it through your head? They're trying to kill me! ... God damn S.O.B's! They set me on fire!"

Sitting there next to me, he pulled his left pant leg up to the knee. Then I saw it - hand sized scorched skin running up the side of his calf from his ankle to his knee. The burn was not yet healed. The raw skin had not yet crusted. I was relieved to see that, so far, it did not look infected. But yes, he'd been set on fire! Young gangbangers got their kicks from tormenting him. He was the downed antelope being ravished by hyenas. And how could he think about art lessons when that was on his mind?

This never-to-be-forgotten sight brought with it one major complexity. If there were no eyewitnesses, how would anyone be able to distinguish facts from his delusions?

In the months that followed, things settled down during our car talks. We got back on track trying to scope out things that could lead to something good happening. That's when I encouraged Sean to write a book. "Sean, there's no way for anyone to know what you're going through, the whole thing is beyond imagination. People need to hear your story...You might have a future in this - sharing with groups as a speaker or something ... You've got it all - personality, brains, the gib of gab. Hey guy, you're even good looking! It would be fantastic for you to share your experiences; you'd be helping people too."

His face brightened as he seized on the idea. That's when we decided to record our conversations. From then on we set a recorder on the car dash and got into it, mostly forgetting that the recorder was even there.

IN SEAN'S OWN WORDS: EXCERPTS FROM

RECORDED CONVERSATIONS

In Chronological Order,

What Was On His Mind and How He Said It

The Longing Within, Anger,

Injustice, Abuse, Respect/Disrespect, His Hopes

TRANSCRIPT: "People are just disgusting. They don't care about nothing. They don't care about living right. They just don't. Everybody who comes around me tries to provoke me. Oh man, check her out, check her ass. Or, hey man I got a rock. You wanna smoke. Or, hey man, let's go get this drink, or hey man, this or that ... and it's always something illegal or immoral – and I'm not interested in it. Nobody's comin' around saying hey, you wanna go to this symposium, this convention? Somethin' with class. Where's all that? ...

I'm sorry for being so fired up, but I just came from the Clinic and they're stressing me out tellin' me I'm not paid up, they're lying to me. I'm stressed out...I'm tired of it. Everybody passin' the buck with me. Nobody wants to freakin' help me... If I'm down here (panhandling) with all the tourists they don't give me nothin'. That's when I get tortured the most – with these strangers on the weekends. They walk around me cause I'm homeless and make fun of me. They talk crap to me. One of them spit on me. I got kids three Times younger than me circling around me, messin' with me. . I'm gonna bash one of their faces in – if they keep it up. They're threatening me, literally. I got a right to defend myself. ...

I know. I just want to stress the point that this has gone way too far... Everybody's spinning me around with the B.S. I have no rights at all. I'm completely exiled from America. What happened? I was born here... Everything bad that happened to me up to this point to get me to adulthood put me in a bad situation. Nobody was protecting me then. Everybody wants to harm me now… Funny thing is, I'm still better than a lot of them at a lot of things …

I'm curbing everything down. I got my methadone. I don't do drugs anymore. I might smoke pot, but I don't consider that a drug. That's medication, it's everywhere – all over the place.

… I'm twenty years overdue. If I hadn't gotten molested I probably would've had a wife, a career, everything by now. And that's not my fault. It makes me mad. You can't imagine the anger… the four that messed with me screwed my life up as if it wasn't screwed up enough. I'm not mad at you, Jan, I just got a life that's not so positive …

I'm sorry, Auntie Jan, I'm just really not in a good mood after the way I been treated, you know, not by you, but people are trying to F****** kill me here. S***, nobody wants to let me live. Like they've Xed me completely out of life. But you know what? God already gave me life, and I'm already part of it. So they can't do that. … I pray every day too, unceasingly, out loud half the Time too, because I have to block out the negativity that's all around me. I pray out loud, so I don't have to hear all the crap.

People circle around me. People I don't even know. Have people looked at the news and seen how children react to bullying? Some of them get guns…People better stop bullying me. They'll get what they're lookin' for… I'm sorry to stress you out, but you're the only one who can calm me down. I'd go totally, frickin' nuts if I couldn't get this out. So please, don't stress out. I don't want to make your life any harder.

... Something I was thinking about on the train comin' over ... I'm getting older. I know it's somethin' you already thought about. ... I feel like I might be prone to diabetic. I get these spells like - like this morning the methadone hit me really hard, and a I feel like, I don't know – like I'm about to pass out, like aaa-hagh. It causes a spike in your blood sugar. Yeah. I want off all of it, and then the drinking. I tried to quit the drinking, and I couldn't eat. I couldn't eat. So I know I'm abusing that right now. ... I couldn't eat for five days, and like this is crazy, forget it. I went and got me a twelve pack of Ice House – after the first couple beers I'm in McDonalds, a couple double cheeseburgers, everything, and you know, I'm eatin'. ... It's weird. I don't want to be an alcoholic, you know, but I am. ... It's crazy, but I'm using it every day, all day long, drinkin' my sorrows away. ... I'm gettin' drunk, getting into it with people and stuff. They get mad at someone and take pictures, put them all over the poles and stuff. They could do that to me too. It's scary. ...

I gotta a voice too. All I know is everything seems clockward. Like my mind feels like it's reformed. Like have you ever read the book Clockward Orange, the characters in that? There's like a whole bunch of examples in movies and books and in stories that I can relate to ... It's just like, I know who the good people are. And they (other street people) get mad about that. It's seems like ... I don't know, cause there's so many people in my corner, Jan. That's what's crazy. Like the police. There's so many levels of the way they talk to me. It makes me not worry. Takes all that worry right out. My thinking shifted about the last year. I'm serious.

Like there's a couple officers took their personal Time to get to know me. A couple of them put me in tears, you know, because they care ...They don't come by me to be mean. They're comin' at me saying, 'Sean, you don't have to be like this. You're better than this.' ... I'm very privileged down there, Dude. Oh, I said Dude, I mean Jan. ... I am Jan, I'm very privileged and blessed. They don't give a lot of people as much freedom as they've given me. The Authorities, I'm talkin' about. I know that. I try not to take it for granted.

Do you know how many Times people have called on me cause I'm drunk screamin' and yelling, get into it with people, whatever? And the cops they just come. They say, 'Come on, Oh, F*** it's Sean,' and they act like they're taking me into custody, and they drop me off down the block. They're awesome! They are, they are .... Cause they know that people mess with me. That's the thing that they've actually acknowledged, and they didn't even have to do that. One officer says, 'I know you're going through hell out here.' He's like, 'I know people F*** with you and say S***. Take it as a grain of salt. Just take everything they say as a grain of salt.' In other words, they're saying, we're the ones with the authority, don't worry about them. And that's the whole vibe I've gotten from the police lately. They don't hate me. It's not always the same guys. It varies over the years. There's actually an officer who's getting sued, but he's cool as hell to me. Isn't that weird? He actually cares about me. ... He locked me up once for sleeping down on the River Walk. It's posted, so they can arrest you. They do it just to let you know they can cuff you up, to check you. They do that to the homeless Sometimes just to let us know who's boss.

Even when I was in prison there were CO's (Correctional Officers) that would bring me coffee and things. And I'd be like man, thanks. I wish I never had to go through that stuff, but I know I went through it for a reason. I know who the good guys are and who the bad guys are ... Like at this point anybody who would want any harm to come to me ... I've already been through so much ... That's like you must have something wrong in your thinking, why wouldn't they want me to recover?

... I don't like being like this a ... I feel like a worm on a hook. I do. I feel like a worm on a hook! ... I feel like I've been catapulted into the fourth dimension basically ... I never realized it when I was a kid, I guess, but I was thoroughly abused in the sexual compartment. I don't know, man ... I don't like this position that I'm in. Feels like I'm wide open, and there's been a whole lot of people comin' at me. Strangers, not people I know. See, that's the thing. I know a whole ton of people that love me, and I know I can trust them ... you notice. Like I've been out there ten years, it's not like I haven't been aware, even though I was doing drugs and all that rippin' and runnin',

I've noticed a lot.

… I don't know, I guess I got my fifteen minutes of fame or somethin', whatever it is. But it's not in the best way. People don't realize I have nothing. Look at me. I'm dirty, I'm smelly. I hate being stinky and dirty. I'm so sick and Tired of it. … "

(Pulls a dog-eared book from his backpack, *The Hero's Journey* based on Joseph Campbell's book, *A Hero with a Thousand Faces.* A hero ventures forth from the world of common day into a region of supernatural wonder: unfriendly forces are encountered. Conflicts, tests and obstacles are overcome, and a decisive victory is won: the hero comes back from this mysterious adventure with the power to bestow boons of goodness on his fellow man. According to many psychologists all mythic narratives are variations of a single great story that spans all cultures and Time of origin. Self-integration, balance, wisdom, and spiritual health are common themes embedded in hero myths.)

TRANSCRIPT: " … I've been reading this book a lot. Ever heard of *The Hero's Journey?* The conversation between this guy Campbell and Bill Moyers? I am blown away by it!

And the other day I was reading, on April 26, I actually wrote this down just because it was so amazing. I was reading in this book, Chapter Two. I can find it right now – about how life has been lived by eating itself, feasting on itself. And then check this out. I wrote it down.

'I just saw a crow capture a poor little sparrow or a

chickadee who wasn't quite maneuverable enough to evade it. Abating. I knew they were predatory birds, but this is the first Time I witnessed the hunt for myself. I'm even more astounded that the whole event took place in Downtown Chicago right at the Art Institute. Right when I was walking in front of the Art Institute a crow snatched a sparrow perched up on a ledge. The crow landed on top of the entrance with the sparrow still flapping, soon to be dead. The poor sparrow.'

The thing for me about it is the location because I'm the true definition of a starving artist. God speaks through art and in this case through real life and nature too. I made sure to bring many people's attention to it besides me too, and people who realized what was happening were in a weird mix of terror and awe. Cause everybody on the street, I was like, 'Look there! Everybody, look!'

But it almost seemed, Jan, like the sparrow gave its life. I swear. Wow! ... I need to write more and more. The thing is, I don't want to start writing, like I've written my whole life. I'm tired of losing my stuff. Mercy Home has a stack of stuff sitting in their basement. I write poetry in rhyme form. I've been thinking of this for a while, ever since I went to prison in Florida ...

... I gotta start worrying about my health. My teeth are falling out. I believe it's from the methadone. When I was on the other drugs my teeth never fell out. The last two years I've been off the other stuff and now my teeth are rotting out. This methadone is rough. It's very strong —

way stronger than heroin. They call it "Liquid Handcuffs," and I didn't understand that at first, but it makes perfect sense because it will bring you to your knees quicker ... I wish I never would have done it, the heroin, but I just wanted to know, what was my mom doing?

I wanted to know. I never would have believed that I would be looking down at myself, sticking needles into my veins. I swore I'd never do that because I knew she did it when I was a kid.

And she made me promise. I waited until after she died. I never did it when she was alive.

You know me and her got high together a lot. Isn't that crazy. That's not a typical parent ... but I betcha if I wasn't at granny's' in Florida when I was little I would never have been molested. That abuse happened with the in-laws. If I was at my ma's it never would have happened. Ma had a good heart. She wasn't vindictive. She had a good spirit.

I wanted to be with my mama, but the government came in and gave grandma custody. Ma was trying to take me back to Chicago. We were at the airport and the Cops came and ripped me away. Granny was drawing the check on me. Later, that was the hush-hush deal. She'd let mom have me, if she would still be getting the check. Ma had such a good heart. She never told me about this until I was a man.

It's weird because that room where it happened (sexual

abuse) later became my bedroom. Yeah, it was a lady the first Time. I been messed with a few Times, Jan, at later ages too. It's weird because like ... I don't know... Sexual abuse is so heavy when you're a kid because it fragments your mind, like you compartmentalize the information. You don't consciously remember it. Then when you get older if you're lucky, and I feel like I'm lucky, It hit me like – wait a minute!. That shouldn't happen! That's why I'm this way, this way, cause I mean, you can look at my track record. Normal boys don't pull their pants down and show everybody on the playground, 'Look, here's my penis.' ... why would I do that?

Because I was having sex with an adult woman a year before. You know what I mean? It's just ... I hate it. ... It's almost like, I feel like a - you know – it put a ripple in Time space. I am Time space. Now I can never know from 5 yrs. old on. ... That boy's dead and gone. And it sucks. It does. ... a lot of reading is what helped me. When I was locked up in Florida the first Time they had a really good library. You know, and I was in there reading every Time I got a chance. Reading books. I read a lot of stuff – criminal psychology, and behavioral psychology, abnormal psychology, and statistics, Federal Bureau of Statistics Manual, Diagnostic Statistics Manual, and psychology, you know. Behind all of it, it's sad. There's a lot of sad cycles with this stuff. Sexual abuse period. Like sex trafficking, all of it. I never thought I was part of it even.

That's the thing. I went through my life oblivious 'til I was about twenty-six, twenty-seven. All that Time I thought I was normal. It seemed to be normal. I had many different girlfriends, you know. Almost got married. But, it's just like I did not know that happened. ... It's hard to explain. It's almost like being two people in one life. That's why I'm this way. ...

... I just want to be a good person, that's all. And it seems like it's never been an option for me, you know, and it's getting old. I'm tryin' to be ... I feel trapped with bad people, that's how I always felt. I'm tired of being trapped with bad people. I don't want to be around it. No more.

... I'm never going to get off this methadone 'til I have a place to stay. I don't want to be on it. I hate that place. I hate going there. I feel like I'm getting pimped out. It really does. It's a legal dope spot, that's all it is. I'm going there drinking legal heroin, but this stuff is ten Times stronger than heroin.

I see why they use it. You go there. You get a number. Now the government's got you .... Yeah, I went this morning. I'm fine for the next twenty-four hours. I go through a lot. The hour before and the hour after. My body's grinding'. When It starts to fade and wane out of me I get emotional, get more crabby and whiny - I can feel ... I'm just depleted. Like I'm about to die almost. I try to go without Sometimes ... but I have to go and drink it. ... when I wane and don't have it I get this gag reflex like my stomach wants to come up out of me. But as soon as I drink it, boom! The gag goes away. I hate drinking it, but my crabbiness goes away. Within fifteen minutes I feel it in my face and hands, everywhere, it permeates my body. It takes about forty-five minutes for the whole thing to wrap up, and then I'm fine, you know. I call it my Soldier Juice. I gonna go drink my Soldier Juice. I know one thing, I'm never going back to heroin, ever, ever, ever.

You know what's odd about all this? They tell me that I'm the most active addict that they can remember. And I'm like, what the hell? It's like, little ironies get to me. I don't know. I'm the most active After Care member, yet you guys can't do something for me to get me off the street?

... Why is that man so ... keeps on bending over... I think he's doing that just to F*** with me. I wanna go smash one of these bottles in his face. I'm telling you, that's the only reason he's there right now. ... He's pissin' me off! I've been sexually abused as a kid. That type of behavior pisses me off! Yeah! He's doin' that S*** on purpose! ...

... Now it's Raining! I'm Rain Man. (Joking)

I've had so many effects on my life connected to weather. I feel very connected to weather. ...There we go, not in the city, I can't breathe. All this frickin' toxicity around me constantly ... I don't know. It just feels like I need to be somewhere like Arizona or Nevada or something. I'm serious that's what my body feels. I don't feel like I need to be here - all this smog, fumes, fumes, fumes. I'm sleeping' right in the belly of the beast. I mean it's just like ahhhgh. I get so tired of breathing these car fumes. I do. I actually grab leaves off the trees, rumple them up and rip 'em ...

hold them up to my nose to breathe the oxygen. It's overwhelming. I wanna breathe!

... See now he's being a little more respectful. He's not pointing his A** right at me. There's a reason that man was doing that. I'm tired of these people F****** with me, Jan.

... if they don't leave me alone I'm gonna kill one of them. Yes, I am.

... Therapy? ...

... So what are you trying to do? Don't keep coming' at me, Jan, you got to understand, it's a process.

I did it at Reed Tlone Center (Chicago Psychiatric Hospital) when I turned my self in, long Time ago. Me and Holly, at Mercy Home for six years. The deep complex stuff is already done.

... Nah, nobody gets done cause there's ebbs and flows, everybody's got different traumas ... I'm so agitated about everything. I want regular therapy but everything's all random, Jan. No place to wash or brush my teeth. It's all chaos. That's what I 'm getting sick of. I need routine. The chaos is killing' me. I need order in my life. I need order. You know, I'm tired. It's amazing I'm still alive.

The last six weeks I hear about another homeless person

that I know personally Downtown, that died. And the other day another one of my buddies, dead. Face first in the dirt. He killed himself … We all watch out for each other. We all got troubles. All of us are either drugged or drunk or something. We all got histories of being abused, all so much in common, but we all need money, so we get into it and turn on each other, and the rumors go around. And, 'Oh, oh, oh,' this and that. We got our own soap opera. It's all chaos

… No, I can't sleep. I'm always watchin' … Only thing is I sleep at the back of the hotel, and it's got lights and cameras, so I feel a little safe. But the camera's aren't good for nothin' until they do something to you."

SEAN'S BIRTHDAY
JUNE 28, 2017
THIRTY-SEVEN YEARS OLD

EXCERPTS FROM
RECORDED CONVERSATION

TRANSCRIPT: "I'm so happy you're in my life, Jan, … Thanks, now I got three cards for my birthday and some stash. … Tory, he's a stockbroker, comes by my corner. Says here, 'People suck,' then inside, 'Except for you and me!' … This one's from Phyllis. She works for the Board of Trade, in a wheel chair from an accident. Now she's got cancer. I don't want her to die. She calls me her son, and I call her Mama. Five O'clock she's taking me to a cafe for dinner.

There's a lot of good people in my corner, but nobody seems to be able to do anything. Like, what the hell, I'm dying in these streets …

It's just survival. They mess with me, and people bother me all the Time, Auntie Jan. They don't give me any peace. They love to interrupt my sleep on purpose. They talk around me like sharks constantly. Vicious people all around me, circling all around me. I'm so tired of that … the police make the rounds. It's ironic that I grew up and wait, these are the good guys, and like a … you know everybody's got it so messed up, man, in their head. It's like, the average Chicagoan is my age in the City. A lot of them have been gang affiliated and they have reverse morals. It's bad. It's not good. It's like when you do what's actually right, we all know right from wrong, then you're looked at as weak and bad. But when you do what's wrong, people are praising each other like, 'You beat him up. You took care of him,' or you did this, or whatever. And that's totally backwards. It's not supposed to be like that. See what I'm sayin'? … You nailed it. Big and bad, the badge of courage. It's absolutely terrible. ...

... I just know that everything is going to change. Change requires a prepared mind. I am trying to prepare myself for this - this big change that's coming into my life. I know it is. I know it's not going to be a change from life to death. Not yet, I ain't ready to go yet. I'm kicking' and screaming the whole way ... Something I have a hard Time with is what to do. What am I supposed to do right now? I know what not to do. See what I mean, and that took a long Time to figure out too. I had to bang my head into the wall a bunch of Times. Oh, don't do that no more. That hurts. Metaphor, but, everything's going to be good I think. I don't know, Jan, I got a good feeling. I do.

I got a feeling that things are going to change real fast for me. I'm pushing' the effort. I'm putting in the effort. I'm praying so much every day. That's something that has changed personally about me in the last couple years. I've totally given my life to God. It's like I'm totally relying on God now. I've never been that way before. I always thought I can do this. I got this; you know what I mean? But no, a-a, God, more God, in the name of Jesus. the Bible tells you everything right there like, all you with your heavy burden, come with me, I'll give you rest. ... And that's what I've been finding. I told you that some days the only thing that gets me through that day is prayer because so many people come at me wickedly, with evil and negative. And I just, instead of punching them in the face, I pray to God. 'God, please, I want peace. Get this person away from me, and get this person away from me,' and whatever. You know, cause it's a - it's a city, you know, all up on each other. In the country it's not like that, you know that.

But don't get me wrong, I love the city too, but when you ain't got nowhere to go, it's walls of a death complex. It feels like a freakin' Natii death camp. I swear to God it does. It's scary that some people come to these cities, and they never leave. The walls of the city grow around them, and they become a cell, and then they die. It's like I don't want to be one of those people. ...

... I can't wait to give this stuff up, Jan, because this Time I want it to stick. I don't want to go back to this. I want to let it go the right way. That means no trauma. Not going back to jail. Blah, blah, blah, this or that. No, I want to make the decision, boom! O.K. this is it, and I want to stick with it. In my head I already got it planned out when I get off of this. ... Ninety-ninety, ever heard of that? The first ninety days when I'm sober, meaning off the alcohol, because I'm still sober minded, but I need to do ninety-ninety. Go to a meeting every single day for ninety days, at least. And by that Time, what it does is build strength, know what I mean? That first ninety days goes by, your body changes, mental changes. I'll probably gain more weight, get healthier - but I need to be around like-minded people cause the disease is rooted in the thinking the Big Book says, of Alcoholics Anonymous. We are bodily and mentally different than our fellows. Got to put the stuff down, cigarettes too. I been smoking since I was ten years old. ... I wonder how much silicone and stuff is in my body? Sometimes I think about it like the tar, and the crap, the freakin' sludge. But I try not to dwell on it too much. I'm like, God's got me now. I can't do anything about it. It's too late, like I already put it in me.

... I huffed all kinds of things, Jan, when I was a kid, gasoline, spray paint, paint thinner, carburetor cleaner; all kinds of things, freon, Blade Air Freshener - we'd take a rag, put it over the thing so you don't get the scent, but you get the gas. We were addicted to huff when we were kids, girls too.

We'd sit in a circle and pass around the gas can. We didn't have any weed. Yeah, isn't that crazy? And a lot of us died. Some of those people are dead and gone now. There's one kid that huffed gas and he was dead first breath, while there's kids like me that, huff-huff-huff, and I'm not dead. And I don't know.

The most wicked, amazing hallucinations I ever had were off of gasoline and diesel. I swear. Acid gave me some hallucinations too. I did acid, LSD, but the craziest ones were off of the gas and diesel. O.K. I breathed in. I stepped back and looked at my hands and they melted off up to the elbows into sand. And the piles of sand looked like they grew like ant hills. And then everything became a pattern spread out in every direction from the two piles of sand into snowflake looking patterns. Then it wore off. I said hold on a second, and I went back and breathed in more, and I had the exact same hallucination!

Another Time I had a little gas can and it turned like into a Mario or Luigi character, and it shot something, and I felt it go into my neck. I swear to God the gas can became alive with all these little characters running around and stuff. So then the next thing I remember is coming back. I was sitting in the living room watching T.V., but no I wasn't! I was actually sitting with the gas can the way I started out. Weird!

… I've done some dangerous stuff, Jan. I believe when I die I'm gonna fly, though. I know that. All I know is I got salvation; I know that. God has confirmed that to me personally. I don't need to explain that to anyone. But that's why I want to talk about it, my life, and tell the world about it. I'd like to help change things; my life could help change things.

… Thanks, a good communicator. I've been told that by a lot of people over the years. I think that's one of my saving graces that God gave me.

You know what, I don't think I wanna, can I leave this empty bottle with you? You can throw it out later? I just don't wanna have anybody see it. Yeah, then they're gonna know one was open and 'Hey, come here, and blah-blah-blah!'

… I know! It's my birthday. I got a big schedule … I think

God might have a big surprise for me today, or something.
I don't know. Who knows what's gonna happen today. If I
go to sleep in the alley again. I won't care. … I'll be fine, I
have your lineage, Jan, I'll be fine.

Thanks. … bye now. You're my Mama too! You called me
that last Time, made me cry, in a good way. Love ya.
Peace!"

ICE AGE CHICAGO
November 2018

We sat in the car talking. A winter nip was in the air, but the sun sliced through enough to shut down the motor and heater. Sean snapped the cap off a beer, and like a polite host offered me a snort, which I declined knowing that he would probably need it later.

Everything seemed cozy here in Sean's safe house. It would be a good Time to ask him how he saw himself getting through the coming winter. He'd done this so many Times before. It was brutal and inhumane. In the past during the coldest days, I'd offered him lodging in an economy motel, but he wouldn't go. The people there would know who he was and come after him. And he hated the shelters. So, stepping lightly on the thin ice, I asked him calmly if he had a different plan for this year.

"God's got the plan to get me out of this s*** hole! Sorry for the language. ... You know. ... my lungs, ... gotta get out of here! The frickin' people ... Won't let me alone, ever! ... If I get a blanket, they F*****' take it. The guy at the hotel let me sleep inside the stoop, ... one Time. But that can't happen again, - he'd get fired. ...

My question set him off alright, but it wasn't rage. Instead, he told me that everything was in God's hands, and he'd just found out that in San Francisco there were tent camps for the homeless. In his words, "How weird was that!"

Within weeks Sean had a new phone, traveling money, and a front seat on a Greyhound Bus.

He was fixed on the windows slapping at the wet snow as the bus broke out of Chicago's icy station. When the sun visors finally came down it seemed like the chain that linked his then and now had been axed. He was running free from the abyss, the darkness, his world that had run amok.

A week went by when he called. I barely recognized who it was. He was so upbeatt that he seemed like a man whose past had belonged to someone else. San Francisco was awesome. The people were friendly. He had a tent, and a warm sun blanketed him almost every day. And, oh yes, it was green!

With Sean, my spirit soared. So, I put on three layers, ear muffs, and headed for the garage where I rolled up the big door and fired up the portable grill. What could be better? Standing inside, I watched the snow accumulate while the steaks sizzled on the grill. Finally, all was right with the world! At last, finally. Thank you, God!

MISSING

A month went by, then another, then many. Sean was missing. So I started making calls to San Francisco. Everyone I talked to was sympathetic and tried to help, but finding Sean was no garden walk through a labyrinth where you smelled flowers. It was more like a tall cement-walled maze that slapped you backwards at every corner. There were the calls to Sean's cell phone with the "No longer in service" message, the missing person report filed at the County of San Francisco Police Departmentt, and the "John Doe" inquiry at the Coroner's Office – each a maze of its own. There was no Holly, Mercy Home, or Rose at the Methadone Clinic where you could ask if they'd seen Sean. He was out there somewhere in San Francisco cut loose from any rescue rope that anyone could throw.

Then came a letter post marked January 21, 2020. It was From Sean, he was alive! But it was sent from the San Bruno, CA Jail. The jail psychologistt, told me that in a rage Sean had caused over four hundred dollars in property damage resulting in a felony. This gibed, compassionate Dr. tried to get a competency hearing for Sean so that he could be treated in a psychiatric ward in a nearby hospital. There, eight beds were prisoner designated. At the moment, all were occupied, and there was no guarantee that he would qualify, but he would try. It was another long shot that didn't hit the mark.

Sean did his time and was released.

How long can someone keep hoping for something good to happen when it never does? The greatest sadness is to lose hope. No matter how sharp the edge of the ax, it was impossible to split the chain that tethered Sean to his past. The new man that dreamed out the window of the bus that rumbled out of Chicago's Ice Age disappeared. He had gone missing in the same old abyss, darkness, and his world that had run amok.

LAST WORDS FROM SEAN
ANSWERING MACHINE PHONE MESSAGES

San Francisco, CA

2021

Transcribed in Order Received

PHONE MESSAGE SAN FRANCISCO
Suher Health California Pacific Hospital, Psychiatric Ward
SEAN: (Talking slowly, low and depressed)

TRANSCRIPT:

"Hi, Jan, it's Sean. Um. Just calling to say "Hi." I don't really have a way to call you back after this. I'll call you back in an hour or two before I leave. I'm getting discharged from this hospital today. Ah, I don't know what to say, Jan, my Time out here has been pretty much miserable. Ah, aagh, I don't even know where to begin. Ahhh. I wish I did. Ahhh. I don't have glasses. I don't have glasses on my face. At least it doesn't get too cold for winter out here. Ahhh, I don't know. I got these ghosts from my past that haunt me. All I know right now is I'm trying to stay sober. That's the main thing for me not to pick up a drink, not drink any alcohol, use any drugs. Ahhh, that's about it. I hope this isn't the last Time you hear from me. I love you, bye."

PHONE MESSAGE SAN FRANCISCO

San Francisco Public Health San Francisco Memorial Hospital, Psychiatric Ward
SEAN: (Slurred talking, voice breaking on the verge of crying)

TRANSCRIPT:
"Hi, Jan, this is Sean. I'm in the hospital. It's the 10th. Ah, Wednesday the 10th. I don't know. I don't feel very good. I

don't know what I'm going to do. All this pressure around Christmas. (Crying) I, I don't have anybody to be with. I'm still homeless. So, that's all. I'll try to call you later. Bye."
(No return call. Unable to reach him when calling back)

PHONE MESSAGE SAN FRANCISCO
Zuckerberg San Francisco General Hospital, Psychiatric Ward SEAN: (Voice breaking, crying)

TRANSCRIPT:
"Auntie Jan, I'm in Zuckerberg Hospital in San Francisco. I don't even know what day or anything it is. I'm not doing good at all. I feel totally a victim of Identity theft. And people, I don't know if they're trying to kill me or not. Auntie Jan, I'm doin' really bad. I don't know if this is the last Time I'll ever leave a message for you. But please! Please! Keep track of my life. I'm tryin' to see my Dad in a family reunion and see if my birthday means anything. I want to see you and my Dad together. I'm full of everything (unintelligible). ... I don't know if I'll ever see you again, but I love you. And I miss my Dad too. But you're different sides of the family. Please! Please, try to help me. I'm stuck in the hospital. I'm stuck in this shitty - they're mean to me here. I don't know what to do, Jan. Please! Please try to get hold of me. I'm sorry for bothering you."

AND THEN ...

DANDELIONS
A Final Call

In a lot of ways resilience is like resurrection. You're down, you're up. You see it everywhere in nature, especially in dandelions.

It was about eight months before Sean slumped over dead with the pipe in his hand. Today he called from a friend's phone, the Director of Security at a commercial building in San Francisco. John would put calls in for Sean from Time to Time, to change the subject and calm him down. He did that with bills for donuts, coffee, and Sometimes meals too. But on this day, there was no need for calming down. The two were lighthearted and bantered a bit like brothers. Sean took the phone and talked about how he liked hooking up with John at the building.

But the words that stuck were, "Just want you to know that I'm O.K., and I'm glad you two are still friends." (Joking, John laughs in background) ...

Then John took the phone and said, "Sean just wanted to say 'Hi', so we're saying, 'Hi.' Hope you're doing well, Jan, and-a you have a good weekend. Bye, talk to you later."

When I hung up, I trotted out to the garage. It was a great day to fire up the grill, no snow, and the sun was warm.

Now as I write, I drib back to the ancient voice and that crack in the sidewalk. My visual brain sees the image of the young green sprig pushing through. My mind tells me it's the tiny stretch of green that would get Sean and me through the Ice Age.

But time has passed, things are different now. Sean is the ancient voice.

And there I saw him, the trampled, limp on its side filling the crack in the sidewalk. But he wasn't broken or lifeless! He was still green, and sturdy as a dandelion lying in wait for the next touch of rain and sun.

GRATITUDE AND INVITATION

Warm and heartfelt gratitude to you who have read this book. You are the ones whose strength of compassion and caring holds up the world when it tilts. You are the responders to those in need who cannot help themselves. You connect tragedy with hope.

What if our homeless, addicted, mentally ill had a place to lay their heads that was soft, safe, and quiet? A place with no more dumpster food or handouts to mute one's dignity? A place free of threat with people to talk to and professionals to help heal troubled minds?

A pipe dream? Not so fast. Consider the moral and economic tradeoffs these facilities would bring. Just ask any shopkeeper on the street in San Francisco where Sean died i.e. the owners and employees who lost their businesses and livelihoods due to the perceived human blight lying on the streets and in their doorways.

The question is, can we put our compassion on our shoulders and run head-long into the fray of this moral and economic implosion?

Each of us alone is a drop of rain on a tin roof. But together we can be a storm pelting that roof until a raucous noise sounds an alarm.

Through the years some wise women taught me how to evolve ideas like *The Strategy of the Big Brown Envelope* (12-13).

Startling vivid rituals, I learned, are the only ones that have psychic effect and shock us into the realization that saying is not enough. We must do too.

So, I invite you to join me in ritual. Amplify Sean's voice and the voices of all whom he represents.

With me, slip the book into an envelope. Address it to someone who is networked and contributes to the lives of others. At the Post Office, join me in sending it down the chute.

> "This one's for you, Sean, and for all whom you represent. Maybe we'll get lucky, and someone will pull branches from that systemic log jam so It can flow into something good."

Jan Cosmos 2023

JAN COSMOS believes that she has learned the most and received immeasurable gibs from having been an educator for over forty years. Teaching has taken her from Chicago Area Schools, to Peace Corp Asia, to Northeast Wisconsin Technical College, and Viterbo University in Wisconsin. There she taught Communications in the Graduate Studies Department of Education where she created classes in *Visual Arts for Teaching and Learning.* Through the years, an underlying challenge for her students emerged. *"So, you know something, wonderful! Now show me how you can communicate it so that it contributes to your own growth and to that of others"* – a lesson learned from her undergraduate years at Alverno College, Milwaukee. Along the way, she was awarded a Golden Apple Award for Excellence in Teaching, received an honorary sabbatical to Northwestern University, and as a participant in seminars with Education Department Faculty, was designated a Visiting Scholar. Later, she was awarded a Research Assistantship at Loyola University Chicago where she received an M.A in Anthropology. Currently, she presents workshops designed to "Educate, Inspire, and Uplift."

The tragic death of her nephew, Sean Messer, brought her face to face with the devastating realities of homelessness, addiction, and mental illness. Thus, evolved this book. "This humble little book," she says, "won't win any literary prities, but the hope is that it will build the kind of awareness that can't be ignored. Awareness is critical, since it's the first step toward change. Without that first step, we are tethered, and incapable of moving forward."